CW01668887

An Invitation

This is one of a range of books being published by **the space between.**

Our books are just one way in which you can engage with the wisdom of our partners. There are many other ways and we want to invite you to take the first step to opening the door to a world of opportunity.

The opportunity to engage with us in many different ways will provide you with an array of possibilities of how you can pay attention to your own and your organisations growth and well being.

Take the first step now by visiting our web site

www.thespacebetween.com

Or call us on

01981 580040

For enquiries in Australia email **ozoffice@thespacebetween.com**
or call **(0) 2 9545 1504**

Creativity

Trevor Bentley

Second Edition

the space between publishing

Gloucestershire England

Published by
the space between publishing
Upper Steanbridge Mill
Slad, Stroud
Gloucestershire, GL6 7QE
England
Telephone: 01981 580040   Fax: 01981 580030
Website: www.thespacebetween.com

ORDERING INFORMATION

Individual sales: All publications can be ordered direct from **the space between publishing**, contact details above.

Quantity sales: Special discounts are available on quantity purchases by corporations, associations and others. For details contact 'Special Sales' at **the space between publishing** address above.

Trade purchases: Trade prices are available for bookshop sales. For details contact 'Trade Purchases' at **the space between publishing** address above.

Based on an original book by Elaine Biech, The ASTD Trainers Sourcebook: Creativity and Innovation, 0-07-053445-4
McGraw Hill, New York, 1996

Printed on acid-free paper
Second Edition

A catalogue record for this book is available from the British Library

Cover design and typesetting by Waimanu Creative Design
Printed and bound in Great Britain by Bookcraft, Midsomer Norton, Bath

CONTENTS

Exercises

Trevor John Bentley

Trevor is a founding partner of **the space between** and describes himself as a Corporate Spellcracker. In this role his fun and joy is in working with Chief Executives and executive teams to crack the spells that keep them "spell" bound in old inappropriate practices. He has a compelling and creative approach to his work with individuals and groups. He loves the challenge of scepticism and cynicism with which he is often presented.

In his work as a coach he balances personal and professional development, because he believes that you can't have one without the other. He works engagingly with metaphor and storytelling and delights in challenging old patterns. He loves the process of exploration and experiment which are features of his work. My new book 'A Touch of Magic' describes how he works with clients in the space between order and chaos and helps them to look at their world in radically new ways.

As with all the partners and associate partners of **the space between** he has trained in the practice of Gestalt as a philosophy of life, and he now co-leads the Gestalt in Organisations programme. Trevor has an extensive business background having worked as a director of a Plc. and as a 'trouble shooter' for a large UK conglomerate. He is an independent thinker, and has a PhD in organisational development. Trevor has written over 30 books on business and related topics, including, *Facilitation, The Parsifal Stories (The Art of Executive Coaching) and Teamwork.*

You will find a blank page at the end of every chapter. This is a creative challenge for you to see how you can use this space to imaginatively support your learning. The 'blank page' is often a major creative block for writers and artists, it need not be - the key is to..... well - be creative.

Chapter 1

Introduction To Creativity

Introduction

This book is about creativity so it won't surprise you to discover that we try to practise what we preach by being creative in how we present and describe the ideas to you. We imagine that your aim in buying this book is to help other people become more creative. To do this you will have to become creative yourself. Some of the things you will find in this book are:

- Misspelling of 'right' (wright for right, because wrong begins with a 'w'. Do you need a better reason?).
- Instructions that appear to be incomplete thus enabling your team to be creative in their interpretation.
- No ground rules, because rules - self-imposed or otherwise - are some of the greatest inhibitors of creativity; and you will see your team making up their own rules so they can feel more comfortable.
- We invite you to use playdoh, crayons and toys that will help to get in touch with the creative child in each of us.
- We also suggest using music to enliven all your senses which we need to be truly creative.
- There are no margin notes in this book because it is about creativity. We believe you will use the margins to create your own notes and key points.

The Importance Of Your Creativity

In working with this material to sharpen your team's skills you have to call on all of your own creativity, both in using the materials and how you relate them to the specific personal and corporate needs that you and your team may have.

It is important that you model creative ways of working and participate with your team in this learning experience. The aim is to increase your and their 'creativity spectrum', i.e. the range of ways in which you are able to be creative.

For example, be creative in the way that you customize materials to fit your culture and your team's needs. Be creative in the way that you organize the learning activities and bring your team together to explore and learn about creativity.

Maintaining The Creative Impact

Here are some creative ideas for how you can follow up your creativity learning with your team.

- Hold a follow-up lunch and bring along some of the more memorable elements of the learning that you have all done together.
- Hold a family night in which you have some mini-creativity exercises, have a toy table, invite your team to co-ordinate the event.
- Take pictures of the learning events and display them on the notice board, as well as sending team members copies.
- Invite team members to share their creative learning and experiences with a colleague and create a creative partnership.
- Have your team members start a journal and provide journals at the completion of the learning.
- Start a creativity group where team members meet once a week to share how they are using creativity to contribute to family, community, company or world.
- Provide a list of creativity books, or create a 'creativity library'.

Creativity only stops when we shut the door and draw the curtains. It is our natural humanness to be creative and adaptable.

Coming To Your Senses

Creativity is enhanced by stimuli to the brain. What stimulates us varies from person to person. In any learning activity the more senses that can be brought in to play the better. This is particularly important when people are learning about creativity.

Here are a few ideas. Add to these as you develop the learning with your team.

Sight

- Display artwork, use bright colours.
- Use special effects.
- Prepare displays, use props and models.

Hearing

- Play background music on tapes.
- Have musical instruments available.
- Encourage people to explore and develop their interest in sound.
- Experiment with a different tone of voice.

Touch

- Have materials available that are rough, smooth, hot, cold, etc.
- Soft clay is good for people to handle.
- Have a sand table, face paints, etc.

Taste

- Take time to plan a unique meal and have a wide variety of food and drink available during breaks.
- Invite team members to bring along 'taste experiences' for other people to try.

Smell

- Use scented candles and incense sticks.
- Invite people to bring examples of smells they like, or don't like.
- Go outside.

Using This Book Creatively

You and your team will get the most benefit from this book if you spend some time exploring the material yourself and then make up your own creative ideas about how to use it.

Remember that it is important to model your own creativity and to be yourself.

The key to successful learning is when people work together co-operatively, which can include being playfully competitive, in a climate that is safe and protective if challenging. It is important for you to bring a human TOUCH, where 'touch' stands for:

Trust
Openness
Understanding
Consideration
Honesty

Chapter 2

Why Creativity?

Businesses Need Creativity

Seems like all companies have recently gone mad! Why?

If your company is like most, you are going through many changes. Your company may have recently invested in new technology. It may have plans to broaden its customer base. It may be expanding into foreign countries. It may have redesigned the business processes by which it operates. It may have flattened, delayered, teamed, re-engineered, process improved or reorganized.

It changed and along with that change comes problems new problems that require new solutions and new ways of thinking. It requires creativity to spawn the ideas and risk taking to push the ideas to innovative results.

A company can no longer survive by staying in its present state. Dr Edward de Bono, creativity educator says (1992):

> **As competition intensifies, so does the need for creative thinking. It is no longer enough to do the same thing better. It is no longer enough to be efficient and solve problems. Far more is needed. Business needs creativity both on the strategic level and on the front line to make the shift that competitive business demands - from administration to true entrepreneurship.**

Companies must become more competitive. How? To increase the competitive advantage, companies can decrease costs, increase quality, increase speed or master innovation. The changes implemented by most companies address the first three, but not usually the last. In addition, most companies are experiencing less than half the potential of the first three if the changed workplace does not encourage creativity and reward risk taking.

> **Even when you're on the right track, you'll get run over if you just sit there.**
>
> Will Rogers

Today, managers must do more than just develop a new product or improve, efficiency. They must also be creative in how they get people to work together in teams and handle the people issues in organizations. They must create a climate in which creativity and risk taking are stimulated and rewarded and mistakes are viewed as something to be learned from and not criticized. Managers must strive to create an OPENED environment.

Establishing A Creative Climate

People are creative not organizations. A company may be seen as a creative entity because it fosters creativity in its people. Generally, a creative company like 3M has created a climate that supports creative thinking. This climate would be, OPENED, i.e.:

Open-minded
Perceptive
Equal
Nurturing
Encouraging
Descriptive

Open-Minded

It encourages flexibility, and creativity. It probably allows employees to experiment with using creative approaches and techniques. Creative efforts are included in the budget. New ideas are listened to without being judged, i.e. given a fair chance.

Perceptive

The company sees things from the employees' viewpoint. There is an assurance that the work is rewarding both in a professional and a personal way. A participative atmosphere is encouraged by asking for and acting upon employees' input.

Equal

People are respected for the diversity each brings. Leadership techniques and styles are individualized to fit the needs of each person. People's ideas are implemented well.

Nurturing

Free expression of ideas is stimulated. People are provided with knowledge through training and other learning activities that provide input for creativity.

Encouraging

People are encouraged to find creativity, different answers. Not only are creative efforts rewarded and reinforced, but time is built in to allow people to be creative. Freedom and opportunity for self-expression exist.

Descriptive

Communication is very good. Clear objectives and specific feedback are basic to everything the organization does. People have frequent direct customer contact. There is a balance between structure and an opportunity for creative expression.

Traditional and still typical management approaches of control, the project must be done correctly, by the book, on time, and within budget, will most likely stifle creativity. The comments that prevent creative ideas from surfacing have been coined as 'killer phrases' by Dr Sidney J. Parnes. You've heard them: 'We've never done it that way before', 'It's not in the budget', 'It's not our policy'. Doing things by the book creates an efficient organization, but certainly not an innovative one.

Will I Know Creativity When I See It?

What is creativity?

Mike Vance of the Disney Corporation says:

Creativity is the making of the new and the rearranging of the old.

One thing that is widely agreed on is that creativity is something that can be learned and people's creative skills enhanced with practice. Though there is a school of thought that creativity is something that we are born with. So since we are already creative perhaps the best approach is to help people to rediscover what it is to be creative and to unlearn the things that may keep them from being creative.

The Brain

The brain, 500 million years in the making, is the most magnificent organ in the body. It resembles a three-pound, grey jellied walnut. But what that walnut can do! It has the capacity to take in, process, and program more than 600 memories each second for 85 years. That's 36,000 each minute ... 2,160,000 each hour... and over 51,840,000 every day of our lives.

The sad news is that this remarkable part of our bodies is sorely underutilized. It's there to serve us 24 hours a day, yet we use a fraction of the billions of brain cells available to us. At one time it was believed that people used 10 per cent of their brains' capacity. Now scientists believe we use only 2 to 3 per cent of our brains.

So what's the rest for?

Who knows! There is plenty of room within our brains to expand to more creative thinking. Wake up the slumbering creative genius inside and turn more of your brainpower to your advantage.

The creative thought process is based upon the idea that our brains have the ability to create an infinite number of ideas, combinations and relationships. Like a kaleidoscope your brain can form, reform and reform again multiple patterns. These patterns and combinations create the new relationships we call 'ideas'.

To solve most of life's problems we usually require both inductive and deductive reasoning; creative and logical thought processes. The brain can handle this easily.

Right Brain, Left Brain

There has been much talk about left-brain and right-brain theory. It is true that the brain's left hemisphere assumes responsibility for analytical functions and the right hemisphere assumes responsibility for the imaginative functions. But it isn't that black and white. The two hemispheres are more similar than different, and almost every mental process requires that they work together. Therefore, keep in mind that these are just labels, and that there are no separate compartments in our brains that store or process information that simplistically.

Regions are differentiated in the brain, but the activities are integrated. In other words, the whole is greater than the sum of its parts. When we sit down to read a book our left brain is translating the written words, or symbols to give them meaning, and the right brain is converting the symbols into pictures in our minds, helping us to understand the metaphors, appreciate the humour and provide the feelings for the emotional content.

Exercise 1 - Using both sides of the brain

Here are several sentences. Read each one and create a picture in your mind to represent each sentence.

- The green motor car went down the long drive.
- The large, green sports car went speeding down the long drive.
- The large, green sports car went speeding down the long, tree-lined avenue towards the large house.
- The large, green, open-top sports car went speeding down the long, tree-lined avenue towards the large house, the driver's blond hair streaming out in the wind behind him.

Notice how as you read each sentence the picture you have changes as your left brain feeds its word meanings across to the right brain for it to create the pictures.

Though the brain works in an integrated way it is possible for people to develop one form of reasoning more than another so that we have left-braining thinking and right-brain thinking. We all do both, but for some of us the preference is left brain and for others it is right brain. The key is to be able to shift our thinking pattern as seems appropriate.

Ibuka, honorary chairman of Sony, took a failed project a miniature tape recorder - changed its functions and combined it with headphones to create the Walkman radio. The Jacuzzi brothers invented a whirlpool bath for a cousin who had arthritis. Fifteen years later Roy Jacuzzi sold it as a luxury bath and made millions. In each case problems became opportunities. In each case right-brain thinking solved left-brain problems. Of course the left brain is also useful for solving problems. Leonardo da Vinci was able to help the Medicis when he calculated the parabolic effect of firing cannon and produced a range-finding device to make the Medici guns more effective.

How Do We Become More Creative?

We have to believe that we can be more creative. And that if we are it will be worth while. This is the first step. The next step is to discover the bewildering range of techniques, ideas and tools that can help us to expand our creativity.

In this book we will explore 10 ways that you can help your team to sharpen their creativity skills. They are:

Compare and combine
Risk taking
Expand and shrink
Ask what's good? And what if?
Transform your viewpoint
In another sequence
Visit other places
Incubate
Trigger concepts
Youth's advantage

You will notice that the initial letters of each approach spell CREATIVITY. Using acronyms in this way helps some people to remember, for others it trivializes the material. Regardless of how you perceive this acronym we will visit it again later. All of these approaches, like most creative approaches, fall into one of four strategies.

1. *Visualization* Seeing the preferred future, seeing the ideal.
2. *Exploration* Using metaphors, analogies or symbols to question assumptions and to jolt our paradigms.
3. *Combinations* Bringing various elements together in different ways.
4. *Modification* Improvizing, adapting, adjusting what you already have.

It is possible to use one or more of these strategies at any time to help you to be creative. Imagine that you have a project at work that is due to be completed and you need to be innovative in your approach.

If you used visualization, you could consider what it would be like if you were already successfully completing the project. What would you hear? What would your boss be saying? What would your customers be saying? What would you see? What would your project look like? What form would it take? What would you be feeling? Look back at how you did it?

If you used explorations, you could develop several analogies or metaphors and make comparisons, then ask yourself what these differences mean, what similarities there are or what differences exist. So if you compare your project with baking bread for example, what similarities exist? What is the recipe? How long will it take to bake? Will it have a hard crust and a soft centre? Who will buy it? And so on.

If you used combinations you might combine your project with something related, or unrelated. Combine it with having fun. Combine it with another project that is going well. Bill Bowerman used the unlikely combination of rubber and a waffle-maker to invent the Nike shoe sole.

If you used modifications you might go back to past projects to see how your approach could be modified for the current project. Or you might ask other people about their projects and then modify your approach. You might relate your project to driving a car and then modify your approach to match the way you drive, or then again may be not.

The point of these strategies is to jolt you out of your day-to-day thinking and move you to think differently. There is no one 'perfect' approach. We each have our preferences. You and your team will decide which works best for you.

Often we go through the day on automatic pilot, allowing our habits to rule the day, hoping for the predictable and avoiding surprises. This can be good because we can become efficient and effective. The drawback, however, is that our expectation of how 'things should be' replaces how 'things could be', and this prevents us from seeing bigger, better, wider and wiser. The approaches in this book will light a new spark that may ignite a blaze of creativity and the world may never look the same again.

What Good Will Creative Thinking Do For Me And My Team?

How about making your job easier? Or making yourself more valuable to the company you work for? Look around, what could be improved?

- Communication?
- Processes?
- Service?
- Products?
- Teamwork?
- Planning?
- What do customers want that they don't get?
- Faster?
- Better?
- What changes do you see coming in the future?
- Where are you going?

What about making your leisure time more pleasant? How could you mow the lawn faster, or not at all? How could you stretch your pay further? How could you make your hobby pay? How could you simplify your schedule?

Tapping into your creative energy can be fun and add a positive outlook to everything you do. You will become more imaginative in solving day-to-day problems. You can eliminate boredom, increase self-confidence and increase satisfaction in more creative personal relationships.

How Can I Use Creativity?

First recognize that you and your team have an unbelievable resource in your heads - a fortune in information. Then you can:

Look For Ideas

Ideas that solve problems, help others to make life easier, improve your work. Develop a curiosity about people, places, things. Trust your intuition and pay attention to your dreams. Everything is relevant to you and your life, don't miss any of it.

Build Your Idea Sources

Read books and magazines, the Suggested Reading in this book may be a good place to start. Ask questions, and listen and learn from the answers. Become aware of what you don't know.

Capture These Ideas

Write down your ideas. Once written down you have them and rereading them will trigger further ideas. No idea is worthless even if you can't see any current value, or it seems silly, capture it.

Use Your Ideas

Use your ideas whenever you get the chance. Shoot for the moon, even if you miss, you'll end up in the stars somewhere. Go for the best, expect the best.

A person who never made a mistake never tried anything new.

Albert Einstein

'But this sounds risky', you might say. Success does not necessarily breed success. Failure breeds success. When asked about all his failures in trying to make a light-bulb, Edison replied that he was actually successful in knowing 1800 ways not to make a light-bulb. Author Tom Peters encourages us to 'fail faster'. Not being creative and taking risks is not moving forward. Not moving forward means falling behind.

But I'm Not A Creative Person!

Probably the greatest barrier to creativity is our self-imposed limitations 'I do not believe I am creative, therefore, I'm not.'

Argue for your limitations, and sure enough they're yours!

Richard Bach

The key to appreciating that we are all creative is to accept the premise that creativity is a continuum. It does not belong exclusively to the artists, authors, and investors of the world. Of course most of us will never write like Shakespeare or paint like Michelangelo or invent like Edison. That doesn't mean that we aren't creative.

We are all on the creativity continuum. To move further along that continuum we must first accept that we are creative and second that we can increase our creative potential. The problem with this is that many people have told themselves for so long that they are not creative that they believe it. Breaking out of this personal belief system is difficult, but not impossible. We each need to be successful at being creative. Then we need our creativity to be reinforced. We also need to take risks and to be encouraged to take risks. We need to be inspired to 'fail faster'.

Imagine what might have happened if the following people had believed that they could not succeed because of messages they had been given:

- Thomas Edison was expelled from school at the age of 10 when his mother was told that his brain was addled.
- Grandma Moses was told she was too old to begin painting.
- Louis Pasteur was evaluated as a 'mediocre' chemistry student.
- Walt Disney was told he had no talent as a child.
- Winston Churchill failed at school and was told he was 'dull'.

As a team leader part of your responsibility is to provide your team with messages that move them along the creative continuum. If you get them to the point where they can eliminate the blocks to their own creativity you will open the door to new ideas for them.

Sharpening Your Team's Creativity

First of all it should be fun. A very important part of creativity involves helping people get in touch with their playfulness, wishfulness, spontaneity, stimulation, pretending, daydreaming, and free association of ideas. You could see this as getting in touch with the 'child within'.

Second, it should be stimulating. This may mean considering what you can do to stimulate all the senses of sight, hearing, smell, touch and taste.

Third, focus on three things: getting rid of blocks, learning new approaches to being creative, and relating the learning to their work.

Fourth, make the learning transferable. Creativity already has a reputation of being uncontrollable, unpredictable and playful. Make sure that, as well as having fun, the ideas and outcomes have some practical value. The key to transferability is applicability.

And, finally, your creative work with your team should help them to tap into their own creative ability. After you have finished this learning with your team they should all feel that they are creative and can apply their creativity to the job.

Enjoy yourself, get a little crazy and ... be creative!

Chapter 3 Failing Faster

Failures Are The Stepping Stones To Success

When some people fail they become dispirited and downhearted and want to escape from the embarrassment they feel at having failed. Their self-esteem and self-confidence are badly affected and their desire to be creative and take risks is seriously hampered, if not destroyed altogether.

In the developed countries of the West, especially in the UK, there is an attitude to failure that permeates through society and is particularly evident in education systems. Failure is ridiculed and success applauded. The idea that the will to try new ideas and risk failure is to be admired and rewarded never seems to be given any attention. The consequence of this is that people avoid the prospect of failure and the whole creative process slows down. Yet failure undoubtedly is a stepping stone to success, and we need to 'fail faster'.

Exercise 2 - Times I have failed

This exercise is designed to get your team, including you, to be open about your failures. To examine what happened when you failed and the results of your failures.

You may have had many failures or you may steadfastly have tried to avoid the risk of failure. Whichever it is, pick two occasions when you have failed and complete the exercise.

The times I failed:

1. ....

....

....

2. ....

....

....

What happened?

1. ....

....

....

2. ....

....

....

How did you react?

1. ....

....

....

2. ....

....

....

What was the result of your failure?

1. ....

....

....

2. ....

....

....

Turning Failure Into Success

There is no shame or disgrace in failing. There can be no success without failure. However, turning failure into success demands two things: an attitude of mind that means you are not put off by failure, and knowing and being able to practise the five steps to turning failure into success. These are:

- being aware of what happened;
- knowing what you can learn from the experience;
- knowing what to do differently;
- creating the next time;
- trying again.

Being Aware Of What Happened

When you fail if you are not aware of what you did or didn't do, you will not be able to make any adjustments next time. Learning to ride a bicycle is a good example of how we learn from each attempt to make small corrections until we can ride smoothly and confidently.

Knowing What You Can Learn From The Experience

To make adjustments or corrections we have to know what we can learn from our experience. This can be done by keeping track of things that have not happened before. Things that are new to us are the things we can learn.

Knowing What To Do Differently

Trying 'harder' is one of the most ridiculous things people can ask us to do. What we need to do is try 'easier'. When people say 'try harder' they usually, mean put more effort in or concentrate more or whatever. In other words they mean something specific and different that gets lost when they use the word 'harder'. Trying 'easier' means doing something differently from when you failed. If you do the same thing only harder, you will probably fail harder. To succeed you have to do something different.

When people say 'you need to do better', they mean you need to do something different. But what exactly should you do differently? Knowing exactly what to do differently is the only thing that is really helpful.

Creating The Next Time

To do something differently from last time there has to be a next time. So you have to go out and create a next time as soon as possible.

Trying Again

Then you have to try again, only this time do something differently. Be creative and change failure into success.

Exercise 3 - What could have been different?

Looking back at Exercise 2 for each of your failures what could you have done differently the next time? To answer this it helps to think about what you learnt from the experience.

Failure 1

What I learnt

....

....

....

What I could've done differently

....

....

....

Failure 2

What I learnt

....

....

....

What I could've done differently

....

....

....

Building A Failure-Tolerant Environment

To create an environment where failure is welcome, it is important for you as the team leader to know how to welcome failure and work with people to turn failure into success. It is also important for every team member to have an attitude of supporting and helping people who fail and not one of avoidance and embarrassment. A good way to do this is to encourage people to share their failures and what they are doing to turn them into successes.

People should be encouraged to identify themselves with failures rather than to try to avoid responsibility and point the finger at someone else. A blaming environment is the least conducive to creativity.

People need to know and experience that they can survive failure and grow and develop from failure as they turn each failure into a step nearer to success. Of course they need encouragement and support in this most creative of all processes.

Encouraging People To Take A Risk

Some people seem to go through life consciously avoiding risk, others do the opposite seeking out risk at every turn and some people take risks when they have to but don't seek them out.

Risk is the possibility of suffering loss or harm by embarking on some action that has an uncertain outcome. Perhaps the greatest of all is to risk our lives in some perilous situation; that is one extreme of the risk continuum. The other extreme might be to risk losing a pound on the lottery. Every person's risk continuum is different.

One of the key pieces of information that we need to support people in their risk taking is how they construct their own risk continuum. If one person enjoys risk, the support they need is quite different from someone ,who persistently avoids and fears it. We need to understand each person's attitude.

Exercise 4 - My risk continuum

Ask members of your team to use the following chart to produce their own risk continuum by writing their own idea of a risk at the various levels.

High risk

....

....

....

....

Medium risk

....

....

....

....

Low risk

....

....

....

....

Balancing Risk

With knowledge of individual risk continuums, it becomes possible to help people balance risk at their own level of acceptability. Supporting people in taking risks is all about knowing their capacity to take them and to help them gradually move up their own continuum. What might seem a very low risk to one person might seem a major risk to another person.

One question that helps people to put some perspective on risk is to ask them: 'So if you failed, what is the absolute worst that could happen?' The answer to this question could help to position the risk on the continuum and to acknowledge the extent of the risk in terms of loss or harm.

Our key aim is to find the balance between too great a risk and too little a risk.

The Path To Success

Creativity is like a maze with many possible paths to success. To find the wright path you may have to try many wrong paths that lead to a dead end. You may end up going round in circles. Only through persistence will you find success. You may accidentally find your way through at your first attempt, but this often doesn't happen and if we give up after one failure success is likely to elude us.

Enjoy yourself for a moment finding your way through the maze in Figure 3.1.

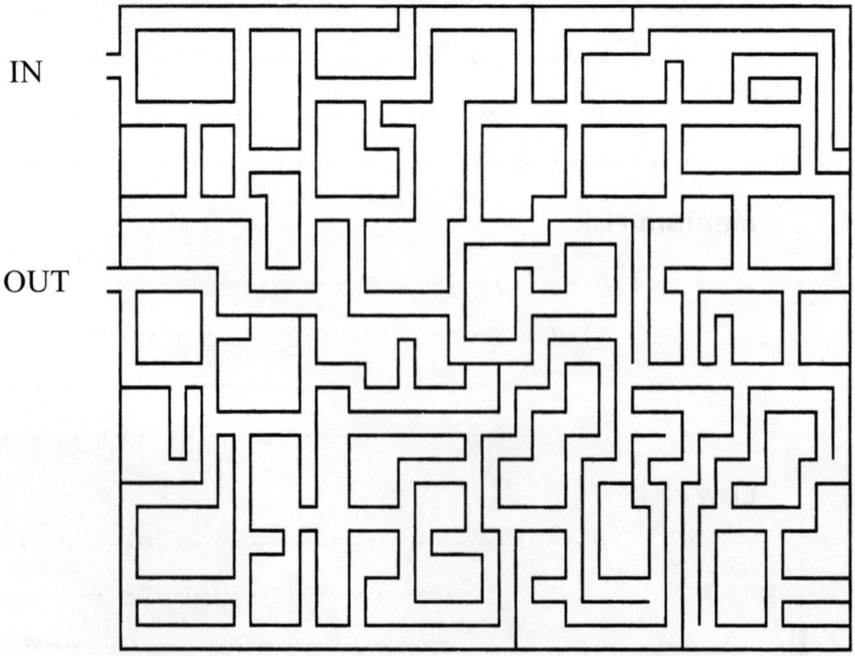

Figure 3.1 The Maze

Conclusion

Failure is something to be admired and repeated on the road to success. The alternative is to avoid taking any risks and to refuse to be creative. Creativity demands that people and organizations become failure tolerant, not in terms of accepting low quality, but in terms of taking risks to try new things. In this process of 'failing faster', it is important to balance risk and to encourage and support people when they are taking risks. The rewards from planting the seeds of creativity will be harvested in terms of innovation and profits in the future.

Chapter 4

A Taste Of Creativity

The Child Inside

One creativity technique is to get in touch with the 'child inside' and by doing so to get rid of some of our adult inhibitions. When we do this it is much easier to be creative.

> **The adults plod along, the children twirl, leap, skip, run now to this side now to that. Look for things to step on or jump over or walk along or around. Climb on anything that can be climbed. I never want to be where I cannot see it. All that energy and foolishness, all that curiosity, questions, talk, all those fierce passions, inconsolable sorrows, immoderate joys seem to many a nuisance to be endured, if not a disease to be cured. To me they are a national asset, a treasure beyond price.**
>
> John Holt

Exercise 5 - Being a food

Bring your team together and invite them to pick one of their favourite foods and to describe themselves as if they were that food. They can say what they look like, what they feel like, what they taste like. Encourage your team to go with this one and if they feel foolish to get in touch with their inner child.

The Combine Technique

Exercise 5 makes use of the 'combine' technique, where we bring together two unrelated objects and we create a relationship that reveals similarities and possibilities.

This technique can be used in a wide variety of ways in order to 'trigger' our thinking into new directions. Use the combine technique to solve this conundrum:

- You are parked on a grassy verge in the countryside. You notice that your car has a flat tyre. You cannot find the car jack. There are plenty of stones from a wall that has partly collapsed.
- For example, you could think about and relate the collapsed wall with the collapsed tyre.

My Creative Viewpoint

We each have a unique creative viewpoint. We are constantly being creative, often unknowingly, as we go about our daily lives. Recognizing and becoming aware of our creativity is an important first step in being more creative.

There are rewards to be gained from being creative that are different for different people. Some will be intrinsic such as, 'feels good' or 'satisfaction'. For others it may be extrinsic rewards such as, 'recognition' or 'money'. Both types of reward are important and necessary to successfully encourage creativity.

Of course it is also possible for people to be discouraged from being creative, particularly in a goal-oriented business environment, where apparent foolishness, or being 'way out', can be rewarded with ridicule and rejection.

Creativity is a process with defined steps. Some of our experiences with creativity have given us positive feelings about the process, other experiences may have given us negative feelings about the creative process. It is not surprising therefore that some of us feel reluctant, if not fearful, about being creative.

Exercise 6 - My creative viewpoint

Share your thoughts together as a team by completing the following list. This will help you to appreciate how your team members see creativity and could be developed into a lively discussion.

The most recent creative action I took was to

....

....

....

What I enjoy most about being creative is

....

....

....

What I enjoy least about being creative is

....

....

....

When I am being creative I feel

....

....

....

Three things that I fear about being creative are

....

....

....

Attempting To Define Creativity

What Is Creativity

- What does creativity feel like when you touch it?
- What does creativity look like when you see it?
- What does creativity taste like when you taste it?

- What does creativity sound like when you hear it?
- What does creativity smell like when you smell it?

Exercise 7 - Examples of creativity

Working in pairs think of some products and/or ideas that you consider to be creative and say what you think is creative about them. For example, the clothes mangle had been in use for many years for drying clothes when the spin dryer was invented. What was creative about the spin dryer? Now think of your own examples.

The Creative Power Of Comparison

Making comparisons using symbols, analogies, similes or metaphors to question assumptions, helps people to break through barriers or blocks and fixed paradigms that they might have. When people do this they open the doors and windows that give them access to the world of creativity.

Exercise 8 - Making comparisons

Imagine a problem that faces you or consider the following problem and relate it to each of the comparisons given below. Allow your mind to make as many and as wild associations as you can.

Problem — The project deadline is approaching and there is enormous pressure on your team when one of your key team members has an accident and is hospitalized and another resigns.

Compare this problem or your own problem with:

Picking blackberries

....

....

....

....

....

....

....

Going on a trek in the Himalayas

....

....

....

....

....

....

....

Painting a five-bar gate

....

....

....

....

....

....

....

Opening a bottle of champagne

....

....

....

....

....

....

....

Changing a car wheel

....

....

....

....

....

Participating in a three-legged race

....

....

....

....

....

....

....

Dancing a tango

....

....

....

....

....

....

....

The central idea in making comparisons is to release your imagination and to tap into the tremendous depth of ideas and creativity that we all have locked away in our minds and bodies.

Creativity is exciting and fun and it doesn't matter if we fail as long as we learn and keep trying.

Conclusion

In this chapter I have invited you to work with your team to get a 'taste of creativity'. You will find that there are more questions than answers, and at this stage I think that discovery is more creative than reading definitions. However, you will no doubt have discovered that creativity can be associated with the following words: 'unusual', 'different', 'odd', 'strange', 'exciting', 'new', 'rearranged', 'reorganized', 'sparkling', 'simple', 'childlike', 'fun'.

Chapter 5

So You Think You Have An Idea?

Having Ideas

We all have ideas all the time. We may not announce them because we might imagine that other people will think we are silly, or not like the idea, or have a better one. Ideas are a vital ingredient of creativity and many get lost because they are evaluated and dismissed before they are introduced to the world.

Exercise 9 - So you think you have an idea?

Do this exercise with your team and work with them in pairs. During this exercise each person takes a turn as the 'ideas person' and as the 'ideas coach'. The role of the ideas person is to have the idea, the role of the ideas coach is to:

- be a good listener;
- ask questions to push for more creativity;
- be positive, always finding 'what's good about it';
- support the other person;
- be a spontaneous, creative, original thinker.

Everyone has the power to play both of these roles extremely well, what most of us need is practice. This is your chance to practise.

No one will ridicule or dismiss any of the ideas that are raised and discussed. You should feel free to let yourself go. Use the following framework to help you:

My idea is

....

....

....

....

What excites me about it is

....

....

....

....

Others will benefit from this idea by

....

....

....

....

My vision for completing this idea is

....

....

....

....

The most difficult part, or greatest hurdle is

....

....

....

....

I'm going to be wildly successful and this will

look like..

feel like..

sound like..

taste like..

smell like...

Making It Happen

Ideas, even the very best ideas, can come unstuck because they are not implemented in the best way. Getting from having the idea to making it happen can be quite a journey. I was once told by a boss that it was no good having ideas that wouldn't or couldn't work, fortunately I ignored his advice. The idea is what really matters, making it work is the challenge and fun of having ideas and can, in itself, be a highly creative process.

Exercise 10 - Making it happen

Refer back to Exercise 9 and complete the following:

My next five steps are:

1. .... Date ....
2. .... Date ....
3. .... Date ....
4. .... Date ....
5. .... Date ....

I'd like my ideas coach to help me by

....

....

....

....

If I run into problems I can

(a) give up

(b) blame my boss

(c) eat two Mars bars and a bag of crisps

(d) beat myself up

(e) call my ideas coach at ....

NOW - DO IT -

CONCLUSION

In this chapter the idea has been to focus on ideas. This is the starting point for creativity. It is about trusting that every idea we have has some value and needs to be released from the captivity of our minds. The doors and windows of our minds have bars of foolishness and locks of fear. We have to get rid of these by using the hacksaw of trust and the keys of faith in our own innate ability to be creative.

CHAPTER 6

THE CREATIVE PROCESS

INTRODUCTION

Creativity may engender ideas of 'magic', 'newness', 'sparks', 'being different', and so on. It means something different for each of us, and creativity is a process. It is a process that can be followed and used successfully like any other process.

STEPS IN THE CREATIVE PROCESS

Creativity does not happen magically, even if its outcomes sometimes seem magical, it occurs as the result of a 'five-step' process. The five steps are:

- Realize the need
- Review all data
- Rest the data
- Recognize the spark
- Refine

Realize The Need

Many creative ideas, projects and products were not 'needed' until 'discovered'. For instance, some came about as mistakes, e.g. Post-it-Notes; others were found accidentally, e.g. penicillin; some came at odd times, e.g. at breakfast a waffle became the model for the Nike shoe sole. In these examples the 'mistakes' were useful because a 'need' was identified. In other situations a 'need' or 'problem' is already identified and the realization becomes: 'What we need to solve this is a...'

Review All Data

The second step is to review all the data available. This calls for research skills, knowing where to locate data, and it calls for people to stretch themselves beyond their normal sources of data.

Rest The Data

The key terms here are 'rest', 'incubate' or 'ferment'. Let all the information available sit and gurgle in the brain. Put it on the back burner to simmer, and let all the creative juices go to work on it. It is like marinating meat in wine. When we go back to the meat it is the same meat but it has changed.

Recognize The Spark

Creativity comes in flashes and sparks. People have to be prepared to recognize it and to capture it in writing. It is helpful always to carry pencil and paper or have it handy, for example, at the side of the bed for making notes of dreams.

Refine

In the final step the idea is taken and refined by deciding what works and what doesn't work. It is like being a JUDGE.

Justify the ideas existence (positives)
Undermine its development (negatives)
Delay personal biases and prejudices (be neutral)
Generate the decision
Execute the decision

Justify by listing all the good things about the idea. What is good about it? What good will it bring?

Undermine the idea by listing all the reasons why it will not work. Play the devil's advocate.

Delay personal biases and prejudices. Don't judge too quickly. Rushing at this stage usually means rejecting the idea.

Generate the decision using the usual decision process. This may include: consensus, expert, authority rule with discussion, majority vote, tossing a coin, throwing a dice, or whatever seems appropriate. It is possible to be creative about this as well.

Execute Do it! Ideas are worthless on the drawing board. Plan the resources needed, anticipate objections, prepare an action plan.

Using The Creative Process

The five steps of the creative process (RRRRR) are a great way to help people to focus on being creative. By following the five steps paying careful attention to each of the steps it is possible to get into the practice of 'being creative'.

Scenario - The intractable problem

There is an office block in the centre of a city that houses 200 staff. Of these 200 people 80 travel to work by car. The car park at the bottom of the building has space for 40 cars. Five of these spaces are reserved for directors. The rest of the spaces are filled each day on a first come first serve basis. There is no other issue that causes as much unrest in the building as the car parking. Over the years a number of different ideas have been tried to resolve the problem, none of them have worked satisfactorily.

Exercise 11 - Solving the intractable problem

Bring your team together and give them this problem to look at. Or better still if you have an intractable problem in your business spell it out and ask them to work on that instead. It will help everyone if they work in pairs as in Exercise 9.

Using the problem as a focus work carefully through the five-step approach. The following framework will help you to focus.

Realize the need, and express it as the objective you have to achieve.

....

....

....

....

....

Review the data, and gather any more data you think you will need. It might help you if you list your perceived data needs.

....

....

....

....

....

....

....

....

Rest the data Allow some days to elapse before you continue with this process.

....

....

....

....

....

....

....

Recognize the spark Write down the spark or sparks that have excited you during the fermentation period. Don't ignore or dismiss any ideas at this stage.

....

....

....

....

....

....

....

Refine your ideas Use your JUDGE to do this.

Justify the ideas existence (positives)
Undermine its development (negatives)
Delay personal biases and prejudices (be neutral)
Generate the decision
Execute the decision

J ....

U ....

D ....

G ....

E ....

Conclusion

This five-step process is simple and straightforward and yet it is very powerful. Perhaps the most difficult part of the process is the actual capturing of ideas as they arise. Many people have an 'inner Judge' who operates to protect them from 'silly ideas that won't work'. Needless to say this inner Judge is an adult who does not recognize the creativity of the child within and immediately stamps on ideas that seem to come from that source. I suggest that you find a way to put your inner Judges to sleep until you need them to help you assess your ideas, and I suspect you will need to call on all your creative power to do this.

CHAPTER 7 IN THE DARK

INTRODUCTION

This chapter invites you and your team to explore ways in which you block your creativity by what you allow yourselves to experience. I ask you to silence your inner Judges and go with the process outlined here. Sometimes it is very hard to trust a process that seems strange or for which you can initially see little value. By going with the process, which is itself a creative thing to do, you may be surprised how much you can learn.

Bring your team together in a darkened room and turn the lights off. Play some soft 'mood' music. Provide a torch for each person and leave them on the table in front of each seat.

Tell the group that you're about to enter a world of colour and laughter, ideas and fun - your own private world of creativity, an experiment of YOU.

Within each of us exists an infinite capacity for creating ideas and nurturing them to the point of innovation. During this exercise we explore how we as individuals have boxed ourselves in, prevented the flow of ideas, inhibited creativity and kept ourselves in the dark.

You may choose to stay in the dark, or to ignite your creative spark. Some of you have already begun to flash your creativity (if some people have found and are using the torch). Take a few moments now to explore it more. You have a torch in front of you, use it to be creative.

Encourage everyone to be creative and wait about a minute. Then say: 'Creativity doesn't just happen'. It is not available on demand though we are all born with creative potential. The success of creativity is a learnt process. You can transform your black and white thinking into colourful innovations.

Therefore I challenge you to begin to widen and brighten your spectrum. Welcome to the colourful world of creativity.

Turn the *lights on* and the *music off*.

The response to this introduction varies, but for many people it is a distinctly uncomfortable experience. This is because:

- It makes some people feel different and/or foolish.
- Some people will be lost without instructions about what to do because they are used to getting instructions.
- It might be experienced as threatening, risky and scary to some. People fear the unknown - they fear failure - they fear ridicule.

Invite your people to express how they feel and why and record the comments on a flip chart.

Questioning Creativity

People question creativity. It is weird. Creative people are weirdos. People are sceptical and disbelieving about programmes that seek to increase their creativity. This introduction may bring out many of these perceptions. However, creativity is a necessary part of our lives, including our work.

But What Is Creativity

Simply put, creativity is a process of taking information or material and rearranging it to form, or create, a new entity or idea. That's all. There's nothing magical about it. Since it is a process, it can be learnt. The steps and tools of creativity can be used by anybody.

The Changing Workplace

Most companies are involved in a continuous process of change. These changes create a new set of problems; problems that require a new way of thinking - creativity to spawn the idea and risk taking to push the idea to an innovative result. It seems like all companies have gone mad! Why? Companies must become more competitive. How? To increase competitive advantage, companies can:

- Decrease costs
- Increase quality
- Increase speed
- Master innovation (which in itself can achieve the first three aims)

The changes implemented by companies may accomplish the first three, but not the last. In addition, most companies are experiencing less than half their potential if the new workplace does not encourage creativity and reward risk. What are the new ways of thinking?

New Ways Of Thinking

- *Innovation* Dramatic change occurring as a result of risking a new creative idea.
- *Creativity* Mike Vance of the Disney Corporation says creativity is 'the making of the new and the rearranging of the old'.
- *Risk taking* Becoming vulnerable or exposed to possible loss or danger.

Creativity helps to conquer the challenges of change. Creativity forces people to view things in new ways. As far as we know, humans are the only species capable of such diversified and complex thought processes.

> **Indeed without sufficient flexibility to permit random creativity in unexpected - and non-preferred - places in the organization, many companies would not have developed new programs, new products, or new systems.**
>
> Rosabeth Moss Kanter

Exercise 12 - Meet the creative me

Bring your team together and ask them to complete the following framework as a basis for describing who they are. This is a right-brain exercise and some people may feel foolish or apprehensive about doing it. Encourage them and tell them that you are going to do it with them. You can share the following version with them as an example or use the one you have completed yourself.

My name is: ....(Zesty)...............................

I am a: ....(Time traveller)...............................

Using the five senses I would describe myself as:

I look like ....(a whirlwind)............................

I smell like ....(a sea breeze) ....

I feel like ....(a bubble) ....

I sound like ....(percolating coffee)........................

I taste like ....(hot chocolate sauce) ....

My latest adventure was:

...............(driving in a Grand Prix and coming second...............

.... behind Michael Schumacher)..............................

Once your team have completed this ask them to volunteer to share what they have produced with the team.

The Ways People Respond To Being Creative

People respond in a variety of ways to being creative, especially when they are invited to do things such as those in Exercise 12. They may respond in a variety of ways, by, for example:

- refusing to do it;
- going through the motions;
- thinking there is a wright and wrong answer;
- sticking to a theme.

These reactions stem from our experiences and background, particularly our early childhood, when we did experiment and take risks. Some of us were applauded and encouraged and some of us were ridiculed. These early messages are the foundation for who we are and how we react.

> **Children are curious. They want to make sense of things. Find out how things work. Gain competence and control over themselves and their environment, do what they can see other people doing. They are receptive, open and perceptive. They do not shut themselves off from the world around them. They observe it closely and sharply. Try to take it all in. They are experimental. They do not merely observe the world around them but taste it, touch it, heft it, break it, bend it, to find out how reality works they work on it. They are bold. They are not afraid of making mistakes. And they are patient. They can tolerate an extraordinary amount of uncertainty, confusion, ignorance and suspense. They do not have to have instant meaning in any new situation. They are willing and able to wait for meaning to come to them - even if it comes very slowly, which it usually does.**
>
> John Holt

People can change; we can rediscover the fearlessness of childhood. We are what we think we are, and we can be what we want to be.

Exercise 13 - How high are you?

Ask your team to group themselves according to height. Do not give any instructions. Remind them that they make their own rules for this exercise.

The point of this exercise is that there is no right way. There are many ways your team can group themselves by height.

Conclusion

Creative people will be creative, no matter what job they perform. To be creative means having the freedom to respond at every moment to your environment by doing what you want and/or need to do. Don't wait for or ask for permission. Following rules stifles creativity. There are companies where the only rule is that there are no rules.

Conclusion

Creative people will be creative, no matter what job they perform. To be creative means having the freedom to respond at every moment to your environment by doing what you want and/or need to do. Don't wait for or ask for permission. Following rules stifles creativity. There are companies where the only rule is that there are no rules.

CHAPTER 8

CAN CREATIVITY BE DEFINED?

A DEFINITION OF CREATIVITY

So far we have offered a definition from Mike Vance of the Disney Corporation that creativity is 'the making of the new and the rearranging of the old'. This is only one definition.

Exercise 14 - Defining creativity

Here is a way that you and your team can explore the meaning of creativity to you by using a right-brain approach. Complete the following:

Creativity feels like ....

Creativity smells like ....

Creativity looks like ....

Creativity sounds like..

Creativity tastes like ....

A Creativity Needs Assessment

Today's world of information explosions, quantum leaps in technology, intense competition, higher quality expectations, shorter product life cycles demands new survival skills for business. Innovation and creativity have been proclaimed as the basic skills required to be successful in a constantly changing world. Organizations that have supported creativity have been touted as models of success in improving performance and remaining competitive.

Most recent literature supports the concept that innovation and creativity are important elements of a successful organization; that they are not just buzzwords, but basic survival skills. Innovation and creativity can lead us down the road to competitive ability and future success.

How This Affects You And Your Team

Corporate growth and renewed emphasis on productivity presents new challenges and opportunities for your business. Sharpening your team's creativity skills will help you to meet these challenges, take advantage of the opportunities and adapt to changes.

Exercise 15 - Creativity needs assessment

Using your knowledge and understanding of yourself and your experiences in the company and your team, complete the following assessment. Use the key below as a basis for rating your assessment:

1 = Strongly disagree
2 = Disagree
3 = Somewhat agree
4 = Agree
5 = Strongly agree

Creativity

1. Creativity is an inborn talent	1 2 3 4 5
2. Creativity can be taught	1 2 3 4 5
3. An individual's creativity can be improved	1 2 3 4 5
4. Creativity is necessary in the workplace	1 2 3 4 5
5. Creativity is linked to productivity	1 2 3 4 5
6. Creativity is a waste of time	1 2 3 4 5

What do you want to know about creativity?

Creativity and our company

1. Creativity is encouraged here	1 2 3 4 5
2. Innovation is rewarded here	1 2 3 4 5
3. Management gets in the way of creativity	1 2 3 4 5
4. Employees are free to develop new ideas	1 2 3 4 5
5. Our competition has more innovative ideas	1 2 3 4 5
6. Our company is a creative organization	1 2 3 4 5

How does your company encourage or stifle creativity?

Risk taking and our company

1. Risk taking is encouraged here	1 2 3 4 5
2. People are permitted to use their judgement	1 2 3 4 5
3. Established practices can be challenged	1 2 3 4 5
4. Failure and mistakes are acceptable	1 2 3 4 5
5. Unconventional ideas get a fair hearing	1 2 3 4 5

What must be changed here to increase risk taking?

Creativity and you

1. I enjoy looking for new ways to do things	1 2 3 4 5
2. I wish I had more time to be creative	1 2 3 4 5
3. I would like to increase my creative abilities	1 2 3 4 5
4. I am willing to take a risk for a good idea	1 2 3 4 5
5. I am creative	1 2 3 4 5
6. Believing I am creative will make me more creative	1 2 3 4 5

Do You Know...?

This section has been included to provide you and your team with some interesting and diverse information about creativity. It will probably create more fun if you ask your team to complete the questionnaire first before giving them the information. See if they say anything about the numbering.

9. That 86 per cent of success in business at any level is dependent upon ....

2. That the supply of scientific information grows over 15 per cent each year, and that by the year 2010 this could jump to ....

5. That Coco-Cola was originally invented as ....

4. That the Nike shoe sole design was patterned on ....

6. That people spend .... per cent of their lives sleeping.

3. That the purpose of the court jester in middle ages was to ....

1. That by the age of seven most children are using about .... per cent of their creative ability.

8. That creativity can be learnt.

7. That by the age of forty adults are about .... per cent as creative as they were at seven.

Here is the information that relates to the questionnaire.

9. That 86 per cent of success in business at any level is dependent upon human relations and creative skills. Only 14 per cent can be attributed to traditional scholastic pursuits.

2. That the supply of scientific information grows over 15 per cent each year, and that by the year 2010 this could jump to 30 per cent. How can we retain all of this? Do we need to? Is creativity an answer?

5. That Coke was originally invented as medicine. Only when it no longer was medically sound did it become 'The Real Thing'. In the late 1800s John Pemberton invented a chemical mixture guaranteed to: whiten teeth, cleanse the mouth, harden and beautify gums and relieve mental and physical exhaustion. The first year he sold six glasses per day. In the 1980s there were 250 million servings sold per day. That is expected to multiply tenfold by 2005 as Coke moves into new markets and attempts to become 'a breakfast drink'.

4. That the Nike shoe sole design was patterned on a waffle. Even though Bill Bowerman ruined his wife's waffle-iron, he found a great idea by using it as the mould for a new type of shoe sole and can now afford as many waffle-irons as he cares to buy.

6. That people spend one-third of their lives sleeping. For the average person that's 202,240 hours. So, why not use it creatively with continuous and focused dreaming? Dreaming and its connection with creativity is a fascinating topic that you may wish to explore further.

3. That the purpose of the court jester in the Middle Ages was to allow the monarch to receive an honest, open view of the world. The court jester didn't concern himself with looking 'stupid'. His job was to take a risk. Why was this important? Perhaps every company should have a court jester.

1. That by the age of seven most children are using about 10 per cent of their creative ability. Why has this occurred? Socialization is a primary reason we box in our creativity.

8. That creativity can be learnt. Creativity training has been around for several decades and it works.

7. That by the age of forty adults are about 3 per cent as creative as they are at the age of seven. We've learnt to box it in. We all have an enormous amount of ability that's waiting to be tapped.

RIGHT BRAIN/LEFT BRAIN

Rather than get involved in the scientific aspects of brain function, it is better if we understand that there are two ways of thinking that can be called 'right-brain and left-brain thinking' which are mentioned earlier. We cannot do both types of thinking simultaneously and we shift very rapidly from one side to the other. The most successful people are those who can shift easily from one thinking style to the other, which is how we can integrate both ways of thinking.

All too often people in business find themselves stuck in left-brain thinking. This is the analytical, verbal, sequential, objective, logical way of thinking and both sounds and is very 'businesslike'. Whereas the right-brain thinking covers terms such as visual, timeless, subjective spontaneous intuitive, and sounds emotional and not at all businesslike.

The point is to achieve balance, or 'whole-brain' thinking. The myth that the left brain is a computer and the right brain a crystal ball can be positive. It encourages us all to experiment with different ways of thinking.

Whole Brain Thinking

Split-brain research has shown that the left side of the brain controls the right side of the body and vice versa. It has also been shown that listening to a phone conversation with the left ear allows the listener to better listen for tone and emotional responses. Conversely, listening with the right ear gives the listener a more objective message they hear the facts and figures and not the feelings. Experts who study body language contend that when people shift their eyes left during conversation they are searching for feeling responses. When they shift their eyes right they're more likely to be looking for analytical responses.

Exercise 16 - Left-brain/right-brain shift

Provide members of your team with a line drawing, or ask them to select one for themselves. Ask them to copy this by drawing it. When they have finished get them to turn the line drawing upside down and draw it again. When they have finished ask them how the drawings they have done differ.

Stimulate a discussion using the following information:

1. Drawing the illustration right side up was a left-brained activity. It was probably drawn one piece at a time, naming them one by one.
2. Drawing the illustration upside down was a right-brained activity. It was probably drawn using spatial, relational and comparative cues.
3. If a participant felt uncomfortable using the right-brained approach (the illustration was upside down) this could be explained by the fact that the participant was trying to use a left-brained approach to a right-brained problem.
4. Usually, the second drawing (right-brained viewed upside down) looks better than the left-brained, or first drawing.
5. Creating the second drawing should have 'felt' different. There is a cognitive shift from left-brain thinking to right-brain thinking - just as we shift in and out of daydreams.

Discovery consists of looking at the same thing as everyone else and thinking something different.

Albert Szent Gyoryi

Conclusion

You will probably feel that you and your team are understanding what creativity is, and that you have had some practice and experience of tapping into your own creativity.

You will probably have identified whether you are primarily a left-brain or a right-brain thinker. It is important to recognize that both forms of thinking are essential and that the key is to be able to shift about and become a whole-brain thinker and thus allow yourself to think more flexibly and more creatively.

Chapter 9

Nine Uncreative Boxes

Why Aren't We More Creative

We have routines that guide us and provide structure so that we can operate on a daily basis. If we got up in the morning and tried to brainstorm 50 ways to boil an egg we'd never get to work. We need routines.

We have developed attitudes or 'boxes' that trap our creativity. We create many of these for ourselves. We box ourselves in with these attitudes. For example, take a £5 note and balance a 10p piece on the edge of the note. It can be done. What is getting in the way for you? How are you boxing yourself in? Now fold the note concertina-style, stand it on one edge and place the coin on the top edge.

Creativity is about exploration and experiment. It is about knocking over convention and established ways of doing and being. This is not to say that the routines we use to function effectively are not valid, far from it. What it does mean is that we should be able to recognize when some routine or habitual way of doing something is keeping us stuck and won't let us free to be creative.

Just as we spent some time in the dark a little earlier, we also allow ourselves to be locked into one or more of the nine uncreative boxes (Figure 9.1).

Nine Uncreative Boxes

Time Trapped

The time-trapped box captures many people. The creative process does take time, just as any other method of attacking a problem or tackling a project. Yet business cannot succeed without creativity.

Environmental Pollution

Our environment can pollute us. If we believe that the environment we work in is not creative, we won't be creative. We could list noise level, lack of privacy, no windows, or no reward as reasons that inhibit our creativity. We see creativity as sparked from outside ourselves. We do not tap into our inner resources.

Risky Business Zone

The risky business zone warns of the dangers of taking a risk. Those trapped within this box view creativity as resulting in weird, unsound ideas. They fear taking risks. For creative ideas to have innovative results, risk is necessary.

Perfectionist Problem

Some people are sitting inside the perfectionist problem box. Here, the person is constantly striving for perfection. Therefore, new and novel ways of doing things are never tried since they could possibly result in less than perfection. Education systems teach us that it is bad to make mistakes. By the time we have finished our schooling we will have taken thousands of quizzes, tests and exams. Getting the 'right' answer is deeply ingrained in all of us.

Calm Waters

For some people, the waters must be calm in order for business to operate effectively and efficiently. There can be no rocking the boat. These people are shut into the calm waters' box. They fear being different and perceive their creativity as making waves. Both the organization and the individual are cheated because creativity never bubbles up. These folks are adept at stating and hearing killer phrases such as 'That will never work', or 'We tried that last year'.

Wright Or Wrong Thinking

Wright or wrong thinking keeps many of us in the dark. There is no middle ground for those of us who do this. But life isn't black or white. Life is ambiguous with many right answers. Creativity lives in the grey areas - in the mixing and matching of ideas.

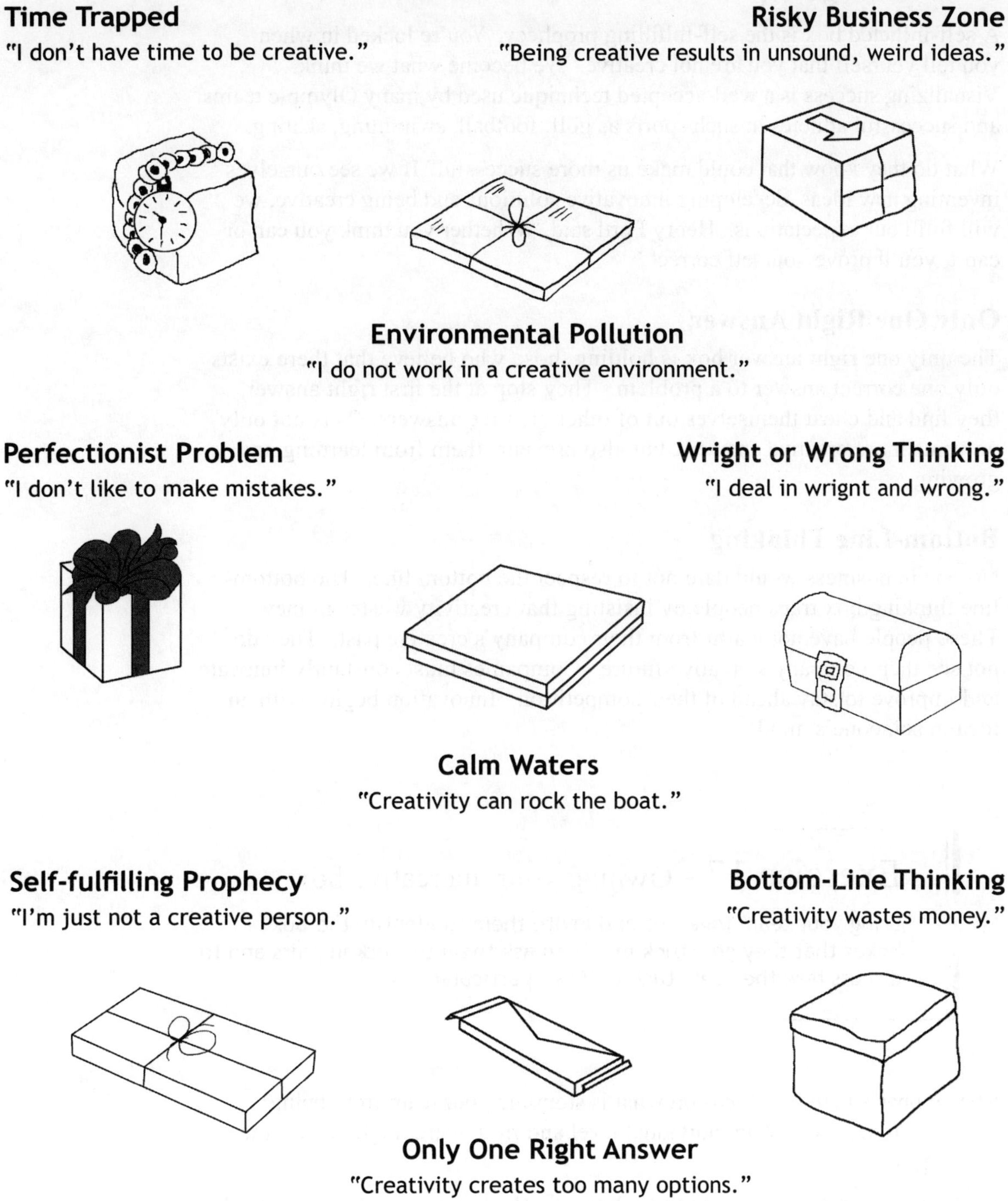

Figure 9.1 Nine Uncreative Boxes

Self-Fulfilling Prophecy

A self-inflicted box is the self-fulfilling prophecy. You're locked in when you tell yourself that you are not creative. We become what we think. Visualizing success is a well-accepted technique used by many Olympic teams and successful athletes in such sports as golf, football, swimming, skating.

What do they know that could make us more successful? If we see ourselves inventing new ideas, developing innovative solutions and being creative, we will fulfil our expectations. Henry Ford said, 'Whether you think you can or can't, you'll prove yourself correct.'

Only One Right Answer

The only one right answer box is holding those who believe that there exists only one correct answer to a problem. They stop at the first right answer they find and cheat themselves out of other creative answers. This not only prevents more creative answers, but also prevents them from learning and growing.

Bottom-Line Thinking

No one in business would dare not to respect the bottom line. The bottom-line thinking box traps people by insisting that creativity wastes money. These people have not learnt from their company's creative past. They do not see their company's creative future. Companies must constantly innovate and improve to stay ahead of their competition. Innovation begins with an idea in someone's mind.

Exercise 17 - Owning your uncreative box

Bring your team together and invite them to identify the box or boxes that they get stuck in. Then ask them to work in pairs and to discuss how they get stuck in these particular boxes.

The emphasis here is to focus on what is stopping your team from being creative. It may start at an individual level and from there might engulf the whole team.

Bring your team back together and ask them, 'How do we as a team get stuck? Which is the team's uncreative box?'

Conclusion

Knowing how and where we get stuck in finding our creativity is the first vital step in releasing ourselves to tap into our creative centre. It is difficult to admit and to own our personal uncreative box, but difficult or not it is the start of the way forward. Once we have identified which of the nine uncreative boxes we get stuck in we can start to think about how we can get out. We can actually unbox our creativity.

Chapter 10

Unbox Your Creativity

Exercise 18 - Unbox your creativity

Bring your team together and ask them to work in threes to see if they can discover ways that they get out of their uncreative boxes. Their aim should be to do the following:

- Tear apart time-trapped boxes
- Rip the risky business zone
- Perforate the perfectionist's problem
- End wright or wrong thinking
- Empty the self-fulfilling prophecy
- Bust bottom-line thinking
- Pull apart environmental pollution
- Eliminate only one wright answer
- Ripple calm waters

After about 25 minutes bring your team into a group and discuss what they have discovered.

Unbox Your Creativity

The only way to release our creative power is to tear down the barriers, the walls of our boxes, that stop us from being creative. Whatever you discovered in Exercise 18 you can add the following ideas, and with this further information your team can practise ways to unbox their creativity.

Tear Apart Time Trapped Boxes

One way to tear this box to shreds is to identify new timeframes for doing creative work. Most of us are creative at unusual times; it might be in the shower, mowing the lawn, jogging, driving or walking to work. We have creative thoughts when we are relaxed, in our right brain. During running or exercise, our brain produces endorphin that accounts for a runner's high. But endorphin, an opiate-like substance that produces a euphoric high, also enhances our ability to be creative. The key is to capture these creative bursts of ideas when they occur. The problem isn't finding time to be creative, it's taking time to capture the creative ideas.

To get out of the time-trapped box, think of 21 instances in your daily routine when you can steal five minutes for creativity.

1.	8.	15. ....
2.	9.	16. ....
3.	10.	17. ....
4.	11.	18. ....
5.	12.	19. ....
6.	13.	20. ....
7.	14.	21. ....

Rip The Risky Business Zone

To rephrase an old saying, 'Tis better to have risked and lost than never to have risked at all.' Children take risks constantly. Adults have learnt to be cautious. There is safety in being careful. This lesson is basic to survival. However, when it is carried too far it can cause the death of our creativity. Adults can unlearn over-cautious behaviour and learn to take, and even enjoy taking, risks.

When was the last time you took a risk?

....

....

Are you a risk taker? Why or why not?

....

....

Perforate The Perfectionists Problem

Education systems, and society, reward winning and the pursuit of perfection. Our whole environment breeds perfectionists, and many top-level people are plagued by this problem. Perfectionism isn't a gift - it's a curse. The one sure way to be a complete failure is to behave like a perfectionist. Poking holes in the perfectionist's problem is no easy job. It takes courage and determination to go against the grain. Many successful people are burdened with an overdose of perfectionism. There are two locks on the perfectionist box. One has to do with the fear of not being perfect. The other is related to not knowing when the goal is met.

No human being can be perfect, but we can perfect how we perform.

Pinpoint your goal
Examine alternatives
Reach out for it
Feel it! Does it feel wright?
Evaluate your progress
Congratulate your effort
Try again

Pinpoint Your Goal

First make sure that you know what you are trying to achieve. Define it as objectively and as concretely as you can. Visualize it and be clear.

Examine Alternatives

Review all of the ways you can achieve your goal. If you do not examine the alternatives, you will not find the best methods.

Reach Out For It

The third step is to **do** something or you will be stuck in refining and researching. To break the perfectionist's problem you must **act**.

Feel It! Does It Feel Right?

Use your intuition or gut-level feelings to assess your status with the project. If it 'feels wright', do it! Don't waste time reaching for perfection.

Evaluate Your Progress

The key word here is 'progress'. Did you perform the first four steps? If so you have progressed.

Congratulate Your Effort

Reward yourself for your progress. The positive reinforcement will help you to break the perfectionist's problem of fear of failure.

Try Again

If you are not satisfied with the results, simply try again. Do not chastise yourself, or quit, or become locked into the perfectionist's box.

Create positive bits of wisdom for the following:

1. To try is: ....
   ....
   ....
2. Making a mistake is: ....
   ....
   ....
3. Falling short of the goal is: ....
   ....
   ....

End Wright Or Wrong Thinking

You have learnt to make decisions, and you are responsible for the results of those decisions. You have learnt to think on your feet and to act quickly. These skills are important to you and to your company. This cannot be diminished. However, one word of caution. Such demanding decisions can cause people to become locked in the wright or wrong thinking box.

Black is black; white is white. Wright or wrong thinking leads to dead-end thoughts. It's either/or, from one end of the continuum to the other. If you find yourself locked in this box, you need to learn to feel comfortable with the uncertain and the unknown.

When was the last time you questioned your wright or wrong thinking? Do you set yourself rules? Ask yourself 'what if' questions about everything you do.

Think of something that you disagree with at work. Now list three 'what if' questions that might move you to somewhere in the middle of wright and wrong.

What if ....

....

What if ....

....

What if ....

....

Empty The Self-Fulfilling Prophecy

The subconscious mind cannot distinguish between the 'real' and the imagined. Visualization is a strong teacher. One of the first studies that provided insight into the self-fulfilling prophecy was conducted with a group of volunteer students who were divided into three groups and rated according to their ability to make basket-ball free-throws. The first group, the control group, was told to do nothing for the next two weeks. The second group practised free-throws for 20 minutes every day for two weeks. The third group was told not to touch a basket-ball, but to visualize themselves making free-throws with 100 per cent accuracy. There was no change in the control group. The second group increased its average by 24 per cent. The third group improved its average by 23 per cent without touching a ball.

The moral? See yourself as being successful and you will be. See yourself as creative and you are. Whether you think you can or cannot, you will prove yourself correct.

At home I've been creative by ....

....

....

....

....

At work I've been creative by ....

....

....

....

Bust Bottom Line Thinking

The bottom line for any business is profit. People only buy what they want or need. The question that this box raises is: 'What place does creativity have in making profit?'

Arthur Pedrick was the world's most unsuccessful inventor. He patented 162 inventions from 1962-1977, and more since then. None have ever been produced commercially. For example, he created:

- a bike with amphibious capacity;
- a car attachment that enables a person to drive from the back seat;
- a golf ball that can be steered in flight.

These are all very creative, but did not result in innovative products, because the interest of the creator and the interest of the user conflicted. Innovation is creativity made usable.

Bust bottom-line thoughts by rephrasing them for innovation. What are the bottom-line thoughts that block your creativity? Write three here, then rephrase them.

1. ....
....
....

2. ....
....
....

3. ....
....
....

Pull Apart Environmental Pollution

There are a variety of elements in an environment that could stifle or box creativity. Some people are more affected by colour than others. If the environment is drab, these people feel dull and uncreative. Many people are distracted by noise, and yet others need noise in order to be creative. In today's workplaces shutting out the world is neither possible nor advisable. Interruptions by phone and face-to-face contact can distract people. One of the most influential factors in the environment is how people's creative endeavours are perceived by others, especially by more senior staff.

If you've been using your environment as an excuse to avoid being creative, you're fooling yourself. Of course outside influences do help foster and support creative ideas, but creativity is generated from within. Identify environmental excuses and devise solutions to overcome them on your own, without changing the environment.

Excuses

....

....

....

....

....

Solutions

....

....

....

....

....

Eliminate Only One Wright Answer

After working for several hours, sometimes days, to reach a solution or answer to a particular problem, it is easy to accept the first answer that is found. Often people become so committed to that hard-earned answer that they cannot see alternatives. The problem with only one wright answer is that it boxes in other creative ideas.

If you find only one wright answer, it's because you stopped looking. Think about it .... Now find other wright answers.

You need more money. You decide to get a weekend job. That's your first wright answer. Think of five more.

1. ....
2. ....
3. ....
4. ....
5. ....

Ripple Calm Waters

One business rule that continues to drown creativity is the idea that one should not make waves. It warns that it is important to pull together and not to make changes, suggestions, remarks, or proposals that will ripple the calm, collected, efficient waters of the company. This attitude has merit in that anarchy will destroy any organization. However, if this attitude stops the flow of creative ideas the company will run aground.

It is important to **appropriately** ripple the calm waters.

Calm waters should be rippled in two instances: outmoded rules and new challenges. Working together as a team list under each category any ideas that may need to be rippled in your area of work.

Outmoded rules

....

....

....

....

....

....

....

....

....

New challenges

....

....

....

....

....

....

....

....

....

....

Conclusion

What does this say?

OPPORTUNITYISNOWHERE

Some people read this as 'Opportunity I snow here', and some people read this as 'Opportunity is now here', and some people read this as 'Opportunity is no where'.

It's all a matter of perception. Perhaps you find it interesting that the same letters can mean the opposite depending upon how we read them? Our view of creativity, work and life can be seen in the same way.

CHAPTER 11 SEE THE LIGHT

A CREATIVE ENVIRONMENT

Most creative people understand the need for a specific environment or routine to enhance their creative abilities. The following people, famous for their creativity, had a strange variety of environmental needs.

Mozart needed to exercise before he composed music. Dr Samuel Johnson wanted a purring cat, orange peel and tea in his creative environment. Immanuel Kant liked to work in bed at times with blankets arranged in a special way. Hart Crane played jazz loudly, and Johann Schiller needed to fill his desk with rotten apples. Archimedes recognized the importance of relaxing and often solved his most difficult problems in a hot bath. And, finally, Samuel Cray of super-computer fame, digs tunnels beneath his house when he feels blocked from creative ideas.

Get in touch with what makes you feel creative. Is it certain scents (the change of seasons, cinnamon, baking bread), sights (sunrise, mountains, holiday pictures, flowers), sounds (ocean waves, jazz music, silence) tastes (chocolate, oranges, cappuccino) or touch (cool glass, comfortable T-shirt, spring breeze)?

Exercise 19 - My creative climate

When people are aware of what helps them to be creative it becomes possible to establish the environment they need. Ask each member of your team to list below what they need to be at their creative best.

I am at my creative best when:

1. ....

   ....

2. ....

   ....

3. ....

   ....

4. ....

   ....

5. ....

   ....

A Spectrum Of Creative Techniques

In Chapter 2 I mentioned 10 creative skills that you can help your team to become sharper. I used the word creativity as an acronym to help you remember the 10 techniques. You might find the use of acronyms somewhat contrived, but I find them a useful and creative way to remember things. Here is the list:

Compare and combine
Risk taking
Expand and shrink
Ask 'What's good?' and 'What if?'
Transform your viewpoint
In another sequence
Visit other places
Incubate
Trigger concepts
Youth's advantage

In this chapter I provide an exercise for each of these techniques for you to use with your team. I suggest you take each one and work with it before moving on to the next technique, and use your creativity in the ways in which you encourage your team to work with the techniques.

Compare And Combine

These are actually two different techniques, but both have to do with putting together different concepts.

Compare is the use of similes and metaphors to explore a topic, problem or idea. How is creativity like a blizzard? How is training like braces? I have used the metaphor of climbing mountains to teach people strategic planning, and balloons to teach people about the economic impact of inflation.

Combine is a force-fit technique that brings different elements together in unique ways. What happens if you combine a wine press and a coin punch? This combination helped Gutenberg invent the printing press. What happens if you combine a refrigerator and a railway coach? The end result was refrigerated bulk haulage. What happens if you combine rubber and a waffle-iron? You get a nasty smell and a sticky mess, and the idea for the Nike shoe.

Exercise 20 - Compare and combine

Compare Take concepts and explore them using metaphors, similes, etc. It can be helpful to use the word 'like' when we do this.

1. Complete these comparisons:

   Memo writing is like ....because........................

   Hiring an employee is like ....because........................

   Completing this task is like................because........................

   Memo writing and .... are different in these ways

   ....

2. Now think of a problem facing you and create a metaphor.

   ....

   ....

   because..

3. List three ways that your problem is like your metaphor.

   Because..

Because..

Because..

4. Now how can these help you solve your problem?

....

....

Combine Take a problem or idea and combine it with something else and play with the possibilities. For example, if you combine floor and perfume, you might think of scented carpets, or vacuum cleaners that spread scents. Identify a project that you have not completed or an outstanding problem that faces you and combine it with one of the following words as a means of 'cracking open' your thinking, and identify 10 combinations.

destiny	**sunshine**	**game**	**wood**
beverage	**travel**	**nutrition**	**computer**
book	**leisure**	**ageing**	**construction**

10. .... 5. ....

9. .... 4. ....

8. .... 3. ....

7. .... 2. ....

6. .... 1. ....

Risk Taking

Successful people are comfortable with risk. The way we are treated as 'risk takers who fall' will impact on our willingness to try again. Do you celebrate your failures as well as your successes? Tom Peters says that failure is a sign that someone is doing something! He also says that companies should 'Fail faster!' Successful people treat failures as stepping stones to success. Creativity without risk is an idea without action.

Exercise 21 - Risk taking

Healthy risks are calculated risks. Determine the pros and cons of the risk. This could be as simple as listing all the positives and negatives about taking or not taking the risk. Will the gain be worth the pain?

How can you become a successful risk taker?

- Assess your willingness to take risks; challenge your assumptions.
- Accept that risk takers are often criticized.
- Establish a firm goal before taking risks.
- Minimize risk by managing information, exercising control and use of your time.
- Be sure you are ready, but don't wait for perfection.
- Size up the resistance, and honour it.
- Break the risk down into manageable chunks.
- Share the risk and your vision.
- Keep everyone who is involved informed.
- Learn to be flexible and roll with the punches.
- Learn from what happens. Always review and evaluate outcomes.
- Stretch yourself. Practise taking risks in all areas of your life.
- Reward yourself for taking risks.

Answer these questions

1. How do you evaluate the risks you take?

   ....

2. How does your boss evaluate the risks you take?

   ....

3. Have others taken your ideas because you wouldn't take a risk?

   ....

4. What do you have 'in progress' that is risky?

   ....

5. What do you want to do about your risk taking?

   ....

Expand And Shrink

This technique is the process of blowing an idea or object out of proportion or shrinking it down to a smaller size. For example, you could expand the idea of window curtains to stage curtains, or shrink them down to a camera shutter. Take one of your recent problems and ask, 'What if this was a problem for the entire company?' or 'What if this problem belonged to a three-year-old?' What would be different?

What do you get when you expand a hair dryer?

A jet engine.

What do you get when you shrink a hover craft?

A hover mower.

What do you get when you shrink a shower of rain?

A shower bath.

What do you get when you expand a balloon?

A hot air balloon.

Exercise 22 - Expand and shrink

Take the concept of delegation and expand and shrink it.

Expand	**Shrink**
....	....
....	....
....	....

Now think of a recent issue, problem, or idea and expand and shrink it.

Expand	**Shrink**
....	....
....	....
....	....

Ask 'What's Good?' and 'What If?'

These questions are critical to opening up our creative vision. What's good about a flood? What's good about being fired? What's good about toxic waste? Engineers at Connoco asked that question and discovered a substance in water that could be turned into a lubricant.

What if we found the magic potion that allowed us all to live to 200? What if the problem was worse - what would it look like? What if our problems were actually our solutions? What if we paid more money to fewer suppliers? DuPont Information Systems asked that question and saved £300,000.

Ask the questions, it's a wonderful technique that will get you through many problems and issues at work and at home.

Exercise 23 - Ask 'what's good?' and 'what If ?'

Ask 'what's good?'

This question is especially helpful when faced with a disaster, when something terrible has happened; your home was robbed, you lost your wallet containing £500 cash, you just messed up your big project. Asking what's good about it will give you a new perspective, new ideas for next steps and a new lease on life.

You've lost your job. What's good about it?

....

....

....

....

Your car has been stolen and found burnt out. What's good about it?

....

....

....

Ask 'what if?'

This question is useful when faced with ideas that are considered sacred truisms such as, 'if it's not broken, don't fix it.' When someone says it can't be done, ask yourself, 'what if?' This is a process for exploring alternatives. Often corporate truisms of the past inhibit creativity and growth for the future.

Identify a sacred truism and then ask, 'what if?'

....

....

....

....

You've been told that you can't change the system ask, 'what if?'

....

....

....

Transform Your Viewpoint

These techniques can be used in many different ways. First transform your viewpoint to someone else. Ask how would the following see this problem. The customer, a circus clown, the CEO, a small child, Winnie the Pooh.

What if you transformed your viewpoint to another time? How would this problem have been handled by the Roman legions? How will it be handled in 2020? How would it be handled the first year the company opened?

You may also transform your viewpoint from negative to positive and vice versa. For example, if you were trying to develop a better way to motivate employees to be creative, ask, 'How could we demotivate employees' creative efforts?' Seeing the other side can be a valuable tool.

You can transform your view by turning the problem upside down. I remember friends trying to get their dog over a stile. I suggested going under the stile, which is what we did by a little adjustment to the wooden fence.

You could transform your viewpoint by writing an advertisement to sell your problem. How would you entice people to buy your problem?

You may also transform your viewpoint by changing the circumstances. How would you approach the idea if: Money was no object? If you were a genius? If you only had 30 days to live? If you were the CEO? If the company moved to the Far East?

Exercise 24 - Transform your viewpoint

It has been predicted that by the year 2005, well over 50 percent of the new entrants to the workforce will be women, many of whom are returning to work after raising a family. How might each of the following view the situation?

- Women
- Your CEO
- Your spouse
- Tony Blair
- 18-year-old male
- William Shakespeare

Think of your current project

Identify different ways it could be viewed and what those views might be from the following perspectives.

Time	Circumstances
• Last year	• Money no object
• 1950	• You are CEO
• 100 BC	• You can set the deadlines
• 2020	• Anything is possible

Change your perspective

Consider the same project and:

- Turn it upside down
- See all the benefits as disadvantages
- What are the benefits of cancelling it?
- You are a Roman legionnaire

The next time one of your team comes into your office and asks a question, ask them to sit in your chair, then you go out of your office and walk back in and ask them the same question.

In Another Sequence

This technique suggests that you explore other sequences: What if you did the steps in the process in a different order? What would it be like to do it backwards? What if the problem was actually the solution? In the insurance industry, what if you got death benefits before you died? Prudential came up with the living benefit life insurance. It pays death benefits to people who are suffering terminal illness before they die.

Exercise 25 - In another sequence

Think about your evening family routine

What if you did it backwards for a week? What are the advantages and disadvantages?

Think of a problem you have right now

What if the problem was the solution?

Think about the information flow in your department

Draw a simple flow chart. What if the flow of the information was reversed? If not reversed then the order changed?

Visit Other Places

Where do you go to get creative ideas? Many people just go for a walk. Most of us need some stimuli to be creative. I am at my creative best watching television. Try visiting some new places to get a new idea, a fresh perspective or just a heavy dose of stimuli. Visit a toy store, walk in the mountains, visit a zoo, browse around a bookstore, go for a car ride in the country, have a long soak in the bath, visit an art gallery, a museum or whatever is different to what you normally do.

When trying to find creative solutions, it is important to look in both usual and unusual places. This demands that you leave your world of business and find ideas in other worlds. Products developed for space exploration have found a wide variety of uses in other places.

Exercise 26 - Visit other places

1. Think of a challenge facing you. Where could you go to get ideas?

   ....

   ....

   ....

   ....

2. Identify a challenge facing you in the next six months. Where could you go to get ideas? Be specific and don't only think of physical locations. What about going to a video, a magazine, a book, etc?

   ....

   ....

   ....

Incubate

The incubate technique simply means that after you have gathered data and information and have reviewed it, you'll let it sit and gurgle in your brain. It needs to be marinaded in your creative juices. This is the time to do something else, something unrelated to your idea. Or try sleeping or dreaming on it.

Have you ever awakened in the middle of the night with the perfect solution to a problem. If not, then this is an experience to look forward to. You knew it was too good to forget, but by morning you did forget it! How can you make your dreams work for you?

1. Before you go to sleep think about the problem. Think about it like a metaphor, the subconscious likes metaphors.
2. Just before falling asleep give yourself a mental suggestion that you will remember what you dream.
3. When you awake don't open your eyes, since the stimuli will immediately wipe out the memory of your dream. Instead review your dream.
4. Open your eyes and immediately write it down. It helps to keep a pen and paper, or tape recorder by your bed.
5. In the morning review your dreams looking for patterns and recurrences.

This process works because our conscious mind can only focus on one thing at a time, whereas our subconscious mind can focus on many things at once. It is the place where information and ideas float about freely and bump into one another, a place of connection, reconnection and creativity.

Exercise 27 - Incubate

Think of a challenge that is facing you. How can you give it a break, where can you park it?

....

....

....

Where can you go to get your mind off it?

....

....

....

Does dreaming of a solution seem feasible? How and when will you do this?

....

....

....

What prevents you from using this technique more often? How can you change that?

....

....

....

Sometimes setting a date with yourself and putting it on the calendar helps. Tell yourself something like: 'Self, I will think about this and make a decision on October 30th.' Then do it! Next time you'll believe yourself and it will work better.

Trigger Concepts

This technique can be easily personalized. Some people have a shopping list' of their favourite words ('serendipity', 'daydreaming', 'waves', 'clouds', 'dancing', 'skiing', 'sailing', 'floating') that they use to free-associate with the issue at hand. Some people keep creativity files in which they keep items (for example, favourite pictures, creative articles, cartoons, sayings) that stimulate their creativity.

In his book Illusions Richard Bach introduced us to a similar technique. Put your dilemma in the form of a question. Then pull out a favourite book and, without looking, open the book at any page and point to any passage. Connect the meaning of the passage to the dilemma. You can do the same with a dictionary or newspaper. Force-fit the word you select to your situation.

You may also use objects. Look around and select an item. How could this item solve your problem or add life to ideas?

Exercise 28 - Trigger concepts

1. Choose two items in the place where you are. Now decide how these items would enhance your present work.
2. Think of a concern you have. Convert the concern into a question. Find a newspaper or book and, without looking, point to a passage. How do the words in the passage relate to your concern? Can you find an answer to your question?

3. Think of something you want to change or improve. Use the following list of words to identify how you might trigger some ideas.

• Mountain	• Contraction
• Forest	• Valley
• Expansion	• Magic
• Green	• Mysterious
• Pressurize	• Shatter
• Holiday	• Dispel

Youth's Advantage

This technique asks you to get in touch with the child inside. Look for the fun in the problem. Your brain is more likely to create ideas when you're having fun.

Playfulness, wishfulness, spontaneity, pretending, daydreaming and free-association of ideas are all things that children do with ease and a lack of self-consciousness. They seem freer to do whatever occurs to them without censoring their behaviour. Edward de Bono found that if he gave children the kinds of problems that industrialists were struggling with that they could produce wonderfully unrestrained ideas many of which became solutions.

Look at your problems through the eyes of a child - the child that you still are. Your child is curious, and will ask lots of 'Why?' questions. Your child will look for the fun in it. Your child will approach it without inhibitions. Try to become a child again.

Exercise 29 - Youth's advantage

This is the technique of seeing things as a child does. Use these guidelines to be:

Innocent	To children everything is fresh and new
Miniature	Everything else is larger than children
Curious	Children want to explore everything
Literal	'Take a hike' means go on a hike
Honest	Children do not filter what they say
Fun-seeking	Look for the fun. Children always do
Positive	Children always see the positive

1. Your team have been selected to pilot a new computer system. See this from youth's advantage.

   Innocent ....

   Miniature ....

   Curious ....

   Literal ....

   Honest ....

   Fun-seeking ....

   Positive ....

2. Think of a 'people' problem you are having. How would a child handle it? What might that child say?

   ....

   ....

   ....

   ....

   ....

Conclusion

This chapter has been about learning the ten techniques to help you and your team find ways in which you can all be more creative. This does not mean that there are only these 10 techniques. There are as many creative attitudes and approaches as there are people, but sometimes we get blocked and locked in a very narrow view of ourselves and our world. The aim of this chapter is to open the windows of the mind and to let the sunshine of creativity flood in.

Chapter 12

Light Your Company's Creativity

The Company's Creative Past

Your company must have been creative in the past to get where it is today.

Exercise 30 - The company's creative past

Working with another member of the team produce a story about the company's creative past. You could try writing a fairy story that starts with: 'Once upon a time ....'. Be creative with this story and include pictures. Imagine you are writing the story for the young children of the company's employees.

Once upon a time..

Creating An 'Opened' Climate

In Chapter 2 we discussed the idea of organizations needing to provide an OPENED climate to foster the creativity of the company's people. The following list of activities (see page 103), which can help to develop a creative environment, is not exhaustive. You will be able to add activities to the list that you know from your own experience help to foster a creative climate in your company.

OPENED Climates

Open-minded — **Encourage flexibility and creativity.**

O

1. Allow employees to schedule their own work and deadlines as much as possible.
2. Allow employees to experiment with using creative approaches and techniques.
3. See employees as creative people by recognizing creative efforts.
4. Encourage total group involvement in creative efforts by establishing work teams.
5. Budget for creative efforts.

Perceptive — **See things from your employees' viewpoint.**

P

1. Ensure that the work is rewarding both in a professional and personal way (e.g. interesting and significant).
2. Encourage a participative atmosphere by asking for and acting upon employees' input.
3. Protect creative employees' from dullards who don't understand what makes them tick.
4. Be a creative role model.
5. Minimize the risk factors and share the responsibility (e.g. giving research time).

Equal — **Respect everyone for the diversity each brings.**

E

1. Give employees credit by implementing ideas without editing or changing them.
2. Enter employees' work in competitions.
3. Ensure that ideas are implemented well.
4. Individualize leadership techniques and styles that fit the needs of each employee.

Nurturing — **Stimulate free expression of ideas.**

N

1. Listen to creative ideas with interest.
2. Provide creative pollen through speakers and other learning opportunities.
3. Foster creativity in group work as well as in individual projects.
4. Provide the necessary climate stimulus (e.g. a creative room, purple office, quiet space or whatever it takes).
5. Accommodate regeneration needs through paid time off, sabbaticals, etc.

Encouraging — **Encourage employees to find answers creatively.**

E

1. Provide the time needed to do so by delaying other work or delegating to another person.
2. Open up resources and avenues for exploration.
3. Serve as a catalyst with actions (not just words) to employees' creative endeavours (e.g. get them what they need).
4. Positively reinforce and reward risks.
5. Allow freedom and opportunity for self-expression.
6. Identify those who exhibit creativity and select them as mentors.

Descriptive — **Give clear objectives and specific feedback.**

D

1. State the purpose of the task in specific-not vague-terms.
2. Balance structure with opportunity for creative expression.
3. Provide input through direct customer contact.
4. Give explicit, as well as supportive, feedback.

Creative Climate Survey

This is an opportunity for you and your team members to assess your company's creative climate. I suggest that each person is asked to complete the assessment and that you then arrange to meet to discuss how people have responded.

Directions Measure the creativity climate that you are working in today

Respond using the following scale

Answer key 1 = Strongly Agree, 2 = Agree, 3 = Uncertain, 4 = Disagree, 5 = Strongly Disagree

	Strongly Agree				Strongly Disagree
1. My work is criticized without letting me explain.	1	2	3	4	5
2. I am encouraged to be as creative as possible.	1	2	3	4	5
3. Management judges employees' actions.	1	2	3	4	5
4. Management allows flexibility on the job.	1	2	3	4	5
5. New ideas are not valued in this job.	1	2	3	4	5
6. Management is open to new ideas and change.	1	2	3	4	5
7. My manager controls how or when I do my work.	1	2	3	4	5
8. My manager understands the problems that I handle in my job.	1	2	3	4	5
9. Management shows little respect or interest in new ideas.	1	2	3	4	5
10. My manager respects my feelings, values and ideas.	1	2	3	4	5
11. Little flexibility exists in the work environment.	1	2	3	4	5
12. My manager protects my creative ideas.	1	2	3	4	5
13. My ideas have been presented as someone else's ideas.	1	2	3	4	5
14. I am respected for the diversity I bring.	1	2	3	4	5

	Strongly Agree				Strongly Disagree
15. I have to be careful in talking with management so I will be understood.	1	2	3	4	5
16. Management interacts with employees without projecting higher status or power.	1	2	3	4	5
17. Management takes credit for employees' ideas.	1	2	3	4	5
18. My manager respects and trusts me.	1	2	3	4	5
19. Management is not open with information.	1	2	3	4	5
20. I am provided opportunities to learn and experience new things.	1	2	3	4	5
21. Management treats everyone the same.	1	2	3	4	5
22. The organization's climate stimulates creativity.	1	2	3	4	5
23. My manager rarely gives moral support to employees.	1	2	3	4	5
24. I can express my ideas openly and honestly to my manager.	1	2	3	4	5
25. Sometimes I feel powerless and inadequate.	1	2	3	4	5
26. My manager communicates ideas so that they can be understood but does not insist that I agree.	1	2	3	4	5
27. My manager makes it clear who is the boss.	1	2	3	4	5
28. I have time and resources to be creative.	1	2	3	4	5
29. Management checks everything to ensure that work is done right.	1	2	3	4	5
30. I am rewarded for taking appropriate risks.	1	2	3	4	5
31. Management cannot admit to mistakes.	1	2	3	4	5
32. Management describes situations clearly and objectively.	1	2	3	4	5

	Strongly Agree				Strongly Disagree
33. My manager is dogmatic; I can't change my manager's mind.	1	2	3	4	5
34. My manager provides appropriate direction and feedback.	1	2	3	4	5
35. Management thinks that their ideas are always correct.	1	2	3	4	5
36. I am encouraged to have direct customer contact.	1	2	3	4	5

Killer Phrases

Killer phrases, as we saw in Chapter 2, can stop creativity in its tracks - bring it to a dead-end halt. If your company is to foster a creative climate the first thing that has to happen is to identify the killer phrases that are in use.

One of the most widely experienced killer phrases is, 'That's not how we do things around here', another is, 'We've tried that before and it didn't work'.

Exercise 31 - Killer phrases

List below as many killer phrases as you can think of, particularly those you have heard in your company.

....

....

....

....

....

....

....

....

....

....

....

....

....

....

....

....

....

Highlight in this list the killer phrase that you use most often when you want to kill off an idea, and be honest about this one.

Killing Off Killer Phrases

Increasing our awareness of killer phrases is only a starting point. If that's all we do, it doesn't help. What is needed is to get rid of them by thinking of creative ways for killing them off and for inserting something else in their place.

Bringing ideas back from the dead could be described as a miracle, so perhaps we can produce a new approach that I will call 'miracle phrases'. These might include such phrases as:

- 'Nice Job, well done.'
- 'Hey, what a great 'idea!'
- 'Tell me how you would make that work.'
- 'What do you need to get going with this one?'
- 'Where else could we use that?'

Exercise 32 - Miracle phrases

Think about your company and produce a list of miracle phrases that you think could be used to replace killer phrases.

....

....

....

....

....

....

....

....

The Road To Success

This is a story about how creativity is blocked. It is an all too true story and like any fairy story it has a moral. I find it sad to write and to read. For some people for whom this story rings true there might be some pain. Others will have experienced similar events and triumphed over them. You might want to skip the story and move on. I invite you to pause and read the story, and then notice how you feel.

Once upon a time,
As often happens in the world of business,
A bright, creative young man earned a promotion.
His new responsibilities and position
Seemed stressful and a bit scary.
Moving to the company's headquarters
Was a big change for him and his family.

However, once he was established,
The bright young man discovered,
That even though his new office was larger
And his authority had broader limits,
His staff members were friendly
And his boss was supportive.
He was well pleased
And he didn't feel as stressed or scared.

Then one day
His boss said, 'We need to reduce costs.
We think you are just the man
To head up the project and meet the challenge.'
The bright, creative young man was happy;
He admired his boss and relished challenges.
Anxious to get started,
He entered his office and began to think.
He worked furiously for the rest of the day
And the next morning, too.
Then, as was his custom,
He placed his brainstormed ideas
On the back burner,
And he turned to more routine tasks.

Later that week, the boss came to the man's office
And he asked the man about the project.
'Well how is it going? What do you have for me?'

The boss spoke with enthusiasm and anticipation.
Proudly the man shared his brainstorming ideas,
And mapped out his alternative solutions,
Saying he'd need more time to complete his work.

'Wait a minute', his boss interrupted,
'I didn't ask for maybes and could bes
We need answers - and now!'
The man sat back in his chair puzzled
By his boss's angry tone.
He admired his boss and wanted to please him.
'You've got to learn to solve problems
Like our other managers do.
That has been our road to success.
Try again and do it right this time.

The boss left shaking his head
And the man put his rejected ideas in the bin.
Soon after this the man visited his daughter's school
As the loving father of a young girl.
He was proud to see a painting his daughter had done.
It was a flower in bloom,
And it stood out from the others on display.

As he observed the class
He overheard the teacher say,
'You will need to change your flower
It has a blue not a green stem,
And it's not like the others.
The petals should be yellow.'
The young girl liked her teacher
And she wanted to please her.
Her father watched her take her
Flower off the wall.

Later that evening at home,
The man spoke with his daughter.
'I like your flower, but it wasn't acceptable.
You will need to do it the teacher's way,
That will be your road to success.'
His daughter sat silently and listened.
She loved and respected her dad.
'Try again, love, but do it right this time,' he said.

After supper she took her picture of a flower
And hung it in her bedroom.
Then she sat down and painted another flower.
This time the flower had a green stem,
And yellow petals.
She worked hard to make it look like all the others.

The next morning at work the man
Was asked by his boss to attend a workshop.
His boss told him that this would help
To lead him to the company way of doing things.
The man liked to try new approaches.
He enjoyed learning new things.
So he entered the workshop positively.

The programme was fixed in black and white.
The leader said it would be followed.
No additions or changes were allowed.
The man waited to learn.
He admired and respected his peers.
Some of the ideas he liked,
Others he disagreed with.
He explored colourful alternatives,
And asked 'what ifs'.

Each time he tried to do this,
A fellow member of the group would help him.
'We don't do things that way here,
We deal in black and white,
It's our tried and tested road to success.
That is the company way.'

At first the man asked more questions.
He tried to find out why and to explore the spectrum of ideas.
But then, each member's response left a mark.
He was learning the company way.
He was a creative, bright man
Though he still liked some of his colourful ideas best.

That night the man helped his daughter.
She had to review a book and she had brought home the teacher's rules.
Together they worked on the review.
The daughter loved her father

And she liked to try new things.
'Can't I paint a picture of the characters?'
The girl enjoyed using her paints.
'No. These rules say to use ink only.'
The man helped his daughter.

'Why can't I tell them what I hate about the book?'
'Because, love, it says to tell why you liked it.'
'Can't I use the computer to print it?'
'It says hand-written here,' her dad replied.
Carefully they reviewed all the rules.
The girl worked hard to follow them.
At last the review was finished.
The girl didn't like it much.
She thought it dull.
But her father liked it,
And she wanted to please her dad.

In the week that followed,
The man toiled over his project work.
He spent countless hours writing and rewriting,
Keeping in mind all the time
The advice of his peers from the workshop.
Once in a while he found himself slipping
Into the old habits of questioning,
Trying to explore the kaleidoscope of ideas that filled his head.
But, being well-disciplined,
He repressed these urges.

He pressed for the untainted truth.
As a final check
He sent his proposal
To some of his peers.
It returned with many comments.
'It's too radical.'
'Don't try this.'
'This is good, it's worked before.'
'You've almost got it!'
'It's logical, black and white.'

He revised the proposal accordingly
And at last he was done.
He didn't really like it.

It was long-winded and stale.
His work was usually like
A fresh breeze in a woodland in the spring.
This was more like a dark forest in winter.
He submitted his proposal a day early.
He wanted to please his boss.

Driving home from work
The man thought about his new position.
He felt more comfortable now.
He had more confidence in himself.
Silently he admitted that his peers
In their wisdom had helped him.
It had been much easier to do this project,
Much easier than any before.
He didn't feel at all stressed.
He felt comfortably calm and quiet.
He was certain he was on the road to success.
There was, of course, no thrill, or electric excitement.
The vibrancy and colour of his work was missing
But, then, so was the strain.
The 'company way' felt more comfortable, safer.

He picked up his daughter from netball practice
And asked her about the book review.
'I got an A,' she said.
'Great! See how well you did?'
The father gave his daughter a hug.
'How do you feel now about the teacher's way?'
The girl sat quietly for a moment.
'OK, I think I really don't feel anything about it.'
'That's how it should be, you know,'
The father explained gently. 'It's more comfortable that way.'

The next morning
The boss called the man into his office.
'Sit down, sit down. We need to talk.
I've reviewed your proposal.
I want to congratulate you!
You've found it - the "company way".
You're on the road to success.'
And the boss shook the man's hand.

'Now we have another project for you,
But we want you to be creative with it.
You handled the last project so well.
Have fun on the road to success.'
And he heard the details about his new project.
He took many notes, but he asked no questions.
He left the office calmly that evening.
He didn't feel excited, he felt nothing.
The new project wasn't really a challenge.
He didn't need to start work on it yet,
After all he knew the company way now.

When he got home
He went to see his daughter in her room.
He noticed the painting of a flower on her desk.
He walked over and smiled a proud smile.
His daughter had learned to paint a flower.
She had painted it the teacher's way.
She was on the road to success.
The flower was perfect.
The stem was green.
Its petals yellow.
Just the same as all the rest.

Conclusion

Creativity is a delicate flower that will only blossom in the right conditions. Creating these conditions is vital for every organization that wishes to embrace creativity.

Creativity can be so easily killed. It isn't clever to kill creativity, it is a form of mindless vandalism. But, then, those who cannot create beauty often choose instead to destroy it. Creativity should and can be cherished. If it is given the right conditions, and if it is nurtured, it will blossom into the flower of innovation and this time the flower might have a blue stem, green petals and red leaves.

Chapter 13

Flash Your Creativity

Brainstorming

In the last chapter we have seen how easy it is to kill creativity. Giving birth to new ideas seems to be fraught with dangers. Dangers such as being ridiculed and seen as someone who rocks the boat. Brainstorming is an approach that actively encourages ideas. The more the merrier.

The more ideas generated the greater the chance that one will prove to be a high-quality solution. The key to brainstorming is to suspend judgement and to ban killer phrases totally. All ideas are treated as good ideas. The nine basic rules used to guide a brainstorming session are:

1. *Suspend judgement* Failure to follow this rule is the major reason why some brainstorming sessions do not produce the expected results.
2. *Freewheeling is encouraged* All ideas that come to mind are valued. The wilder the ideas, the better.
3. *Quantity is wanted* The aim is to have as many ideas as possible.
4. *Piggybacking is welcome* Participants are encouraged to build on each other's idea or generate a number of ideas using a previous one as a stimulus.
5. *Record* all ideas on wall posters as you go.
6. A member may *ask for clarification of a suggestion*. However, it is important to avoid any questions that are directed at 'How?' and 'Why?'
7. *Allow enough time.*
8. *Encourage humour and playfulness.*
9. *Assign both a facilitator and a recorder, who also input ideas.*

The Brainstorming Session

When facilitating brainstorming sessions always remind participants of the aims of the session and remind them of the nine basic rules. It is the facilitator's job to see that the rules are observed.

It is useful to send out a brief statement of the problem to team members a few days before your meeting. This enables them to put the problem on their back burners so that they can incubate ideas.

There should be plenty of stimulators available to the team. These could be in physical form, such as toys, Plasticine, crayons, paints, large paper, building bricks, and so on, or they could be more mentally focused such as word lists, a dictionary, books, pictures, and so on.

Constantly push to generate more ideas. Put a target on the number. Set a time limit, e.g. 10 ideas a minute.

The session could be structured whereby participants write ideas on paper or index cards. These are then collected and redistributed. By adding anonymity in this way it frees up some people's inhibitions. After an agreed time all the ideas are posted and the open brainstorming starts using the posted ideas as stimulators.

Another structured approach is to work in silence with each person having a stack of cards. They write an idea on a card which they pass to their left. When the card arrives from the right, the recipient writes another idea on another card and passes the two cards to the left. When two cards arrive from the night, a third card is prepared and three passed on. This continues until the process slows down or stops. All the ideas are then posted.

When the brainstorming session finishes all the ideas are placed into categories for the next stage in the creative process, which is the review phase (see Chapter 5). You can also keep in mind the GOD principle: Generate, Organize and Decide.

Exercise 33 - Brainstorming

Working with your team, set up a brainstorming session for a particular problem that faces the team at the present time. If this is not immediately possible, use the following problem as focus for the session.

How can we as a team become more productive?

Getting Unstuck

We all have creative potential, yet there are times when we can't think of a thing! Here are a range of ways in which people can 'unstick themselves'.

Do Things Differently

- Visit a museum.
- Take a different route to work.
- Read a book you 'know' you'll hate.
- Visit a building you've never been in.
- Make a phone call to someone you haven't spoken to for over a year.
- Visit an infant school.
- Go for a swim.
- Go for a run.
- Listen to a different radio channel.
- Walk around the block backwards.
- Cross your eyes.
- Visit an art gallery.
- Go dancing.
- ....
- ....

Visioning

- Think about your favourite sport.
- See the task complete.
- Picture the same situation in 200 BC.
- Imagine yourself dancing with Ginger Rogers or Fred Astaire.
- See yourself in a blizzard.
- Picture yourself on a tropical island.
- Imagine you are a millionaire.
- ....
- ....

Word Ideas

- Play scrabble.
- Read a dictionary.
- Read the sports page, or not.
- Do a crossword puzzle.
- Buy three magazines you've never read.
- Look through yellow pages.
- ....
- ....

Get Ideas From The Others

- Hold a crazy ideas meeting over lunch.
- Offer to pay £5 for every idea you use.
- Ask a child for ideas.
- Ask a taxi driver.
- Start talking with someone, anyone, and ask them to challenge you and push you to continue.
- ....
- ....

Get Crazy

- Wear a fancy dress costume to work.
- Have a crazy ideas party.
- Read only the ads in a magazine.
- Watch TV with the sound off.
- Play a computer game.
- Play a kid's game.
- Read children's books.
- Brainstorm in the street with a flip chart and ask passers by for ideas.
- ....
- ....

Become Time-Focused

- Establish a ridiculous completion time.
- Break the task into small parts and offer a reward for the successful completion of each one.
- Work an hour, take a ten minute break. Work ten minutes, take an hour break.
- Set a clock at the wrong time and use it as your clock for a day.
- ....
- ....

Stimulate Your Senses

- Eat an unusual fruit.
- Eat chocolate.
- Use a perfume spray.
- Burn a scented candle.
- Go to sleep.
- Listen to music while you work.
- Touch a smooth surface.
- Go and work in the mountains.
- Go and work in woodland.
- Go and work on the cliffs with the sound of the sea crashing on the rocks.
- ....
- ....

Writing Related

- Use a mind map on a large piece of paper.
- Start writing with thick pens.
- Write with coloured chalk on the pavement.
- Write a fairy story about your problem.
- Write a horror story about your problem.
- ....
- ....

Shock Your Dominance

- Cross your arms the opposite way for five minutes.
- If you are right-handed write with your left hand.
- Start walking with your left foot.
- Listen to the phone with the ear you don't normally use.
- Throw a ball with the hand you don't normally use.
- Read with one eye closed.
- ....
- ....

Exercise 34 - Getting unstuck

Bring your team together and form three small groups. Give each group two minutes to come up with a creative name for their group. Give each group the following different instructions.

Group A — You can use this dictionary. Someone should point to a word without looking and name the word. Then the group generates ideas of how it makes you think of ways to spark creativity. Someone can list them on a flip chart. Your challenge is to get 100 ideas in the next 15 minutes. (Trigger concept technique)

Group B — You should focus on the five senses: sight, smell, hearing, touch and taste. How can your senses be stimulated to generate ideas? List at least 100 things on your flip chart in the next 15 minutes. (Combine technique)

Group C — You have two areas:

- The first is to list all the places you could go to get creative ideas.
- The second is to list how others might stimulate their creativity. These could be famous people, your friends, fictitious characters, whoever.

You have 15 minutes to generate over 100 ideas on your flip chart. (Transform your viewpoint technique)

Lighting Others' Creativity

As you may have discovered in this book the creative process is impacted by two environments - the environment within each person and the environment in which the person is creating. You have an opportunity to light other people's creativity. It begins with your attitude towards their creative efforts. Your choices are to either be CLOSED or OPENED to their endeavours. Consider the following quotations:

> **The best executive is the one who has the sense enough to pick good men to do what he wants done, and self-restraint enough to keep from meddling with them while they do it.**
>
> Theodore Roosevelt

> **There are two ways of spreading light ... by the candle or the mirror that reflects it.**
>
> Edith Wharton

Exercise 35 - Lighting others' creativity

Invite each member of your team to answer these questions:

My own statement about creativity is?

....

....

....

....

Who can I encourage to be more creative?

....

....

....

....

How can I do this?

....

....

....

....

Conclusion

Creativity is for many people a flash in the pan rather than a continuous process that injects excitement, colour and fun into every aspect of their lives. Changing this viewpoint can be difficult because people often don't see the choices they have about being creative. They hear too many killer phrases and not enough miracle phrases. Each one of us can change this by flashing our own creativity like a beacon in a dark world and by doing so encourage others to flash their creativity. One candle creates more light when surrounded by many mirrors.

Chapter 14 Measuring Creativity

Introduction

It seems strange to talk about measuring something that is so immeasurable! So right-brained! Yet people do like to measure things, to know how they compare to others. In this chapter there are two 'instruments', which we have already met in this book, that can be used to help identify the current level of creativity that exists, or is felt to exist in the organization. These are needs assessment and Creative Climate Survey.

Exercise 36 - Measuring things

Suggest to members of your team that measurement can be exact and inexact. Provide them with a tape measure and ask them to measure the following:

- Their height: making a mark on the wall and writing their names.
- The circumference of their heads.
- Their thoughts.
- How far they can stick their tongues out.
- Their normal step.
- Their neck size.
- Their knowledge of creativity.
- The cubic capacity of the room you are in.
- The way they use their left brains.

- How far it is to the end of their journeys to their houses.
- How near they are to each other.

Follow this with a discussion about measurement and invite them to be as creative as possible in defining ways in which the team will measure creativity in the future.

Needs Assessment

In Chapter 8 (Exercise 15) we have already used one instrument: Needs Assessment. This can also be used as follows:

1. You, as the facilitator, can send it to your team, before working with them on creativity, and use the results to:
   - tailor your programme to your team;
   - present the data as part of your information about creativity;
   - present portions of the data during specific activities and create new activities around the data.

   For example, if a large number of your team believed that 'management gets in the way of creativity' you could ask them to brainstorm how to prevent it doing so, or to identify how resources, time or ideas are being lost.

2. Your company may also wish to do a company-wide needs assessment that helps to pinpoint what the company should do to nurture the creative environment.

   The point of the Needs Assessment is to focus attention on what individuals and teams need to enable them to tap into their latent creativity. The outcome of the assessment could be to brainstorm how the needs identified can be met.

Creative Climate Survey

We used this in Chapter 12 as a way of looking at the current creative climate and to see how it could be improved. This is also an instrument that can be used for a whole organization. It provides results in six categories: how open-minded, perceptive, equal, nurturing, encouraging and descriptive the climate is. These six categories provide the basis for what is needed to foster a creative climate.

The Creative Climate Survey provides a dual scoring system that measures the climate from the positive as well as the negative aspect. The positive score is represented as an 'open climate' score. The negative score is represented as a 'closed climate' score.

You can at this point return to the work that was done in Chapter 12, and use the score sheet to assess the climate that currently exists in your company. If you didn't use the Creative Climate Survey when you were working through that chapter, use it now to produce a score, both positive and negative.

Of course you could answer the survey in such a way as to give yourselves the score you want, so I suggest that the scoring system outcomes are not shared with your team before completing the survey. Alternatively you could start with the score you want and see how near or far from this ideal you are at the present time.

The whole point of the Creative Climate Survey is to provide a basis for working towards developing a more creative climate. The outcome of the survey can be used as a starting point for a brainstorming session to see how the positive aspects can be improved and the negative aspects eliminated.

CREATIVITY CLIMATE SURVEY SCORING

Scoring Put the numbers you assigned to each statement in the appropriate blanks. Add them to subtotal each climate descriptor and total your score.

1.	Critical	2.	Open-minded
3.		4.	
5.		6.	
Subtotal		Subtotal	
7.	Lashing	8.	Perceptive
9.		10.	
11.		12.	
Subtotal		Subtotal	
13.	Opportunistic	14.	Equal
15.		16.	
17.		18.	
Subtotal		Subtotal	
19.	Solo	20.	Nurturing
21.		22.	
23.		24.	
Subtotal		Subtotal	
25.	Egotistical	26.	Encouraging
27.		28.	
29.		30.	
Subtotal		Subtotal	
31.	Dogmatic	32.	Descriptive
33.		34.	
35.		36.	
Subtotal		Subtotal	
Closed Score		Opened Score	

Total Score Guide

No matter what your climate or label is, you are now aware of your climate's tone. This can provide the information and foundation to foster improving your creativity climate.

Closed		**Opened**	
18-41	Closed	18-41	Opened
42-65	Neutral	42-65	Neutral
66-90	Opened	66-90	Closed

Conclusion

Creativity is something that is like magicians performing their 'magic'. It looks fascinating and truly magical, and yet it is based on understanding and learning the basic skills and techniques or tricks necessary to perform creatively. Just like the magician, creative people need an environment that supports, nurtures and believes in their creativity and that, though it knows the magic isn't really magic, is prepared to enjoy and applaud the audacity and skill of the creative person.

Chapter 15 Your Creative Style

Introduction

Each of us have our own distinctive creative style. The effects of our upbringing, education, work and life experiences all combine to give us a unique outlook and way of responding to what happens to us, and affects how we behave in any set of circumstances. Being creative is part of our uniqueness.

Exercise 37 - Describing creative styles

Here are five different creative styles. I have given them a name. Ask each of your team to describe the characteristics of each creative style. How would each style be recognized?

Creative style	**Description**
The bull in a china shop	....
	....
	....
	....
	....

The 'Eureka' ....

....

....

....

....

The 'tiptoeing over broken glass' ....

....

....

....

....

The 'do you think, it is possible, maybe' ....

....

....

....

....

The 'I have this idea' ....

....

....

....

....

The 'I'm not taking no for an answer' ....

....

....

....

....

Characteristics Of Creative People

There are, however, certain characteristics of people we recognize as being creative. These include the following, which are based on studies of people famous for their creativity.

- They are a social bunch who thrive on visiting and talking with other people.
- They don't give up and they are highly motivated.
- They work long and hard in their field before they create something for which they are renowned.
- Their early experiences were varied and filled with the freedom to explore.
- They have excellent senses of humour.

There are many characteristics that are linked to creativity and the following will give you a taste of some of them.

- Not following rules
- Spontaneity
- Fun-loving
- Highly sensitive to own senses (sight, smell, sound, touch, taste)
- See what others don't see
- Action oriented
- Push beyond obstacles
- Not content with the obvious
- Highly differentiated
- Enthusiastic verging on the evangelical
- Highly motivated
- High level of self-belief and of self-esteem

Exercise 38 - Your creative style

Work with your team and ask each person to list the attributes they have that:

- contribute to their creativity;
- get in the way of their creativity.

Ask everyone to be as open and honest as they possibly can be in doing this exercise.

Attributes that:

Contribute	**Get in the way**
....	....
....	....
....	....
....	....

Contribute	**Get in the way**
....	....
....	....
....	....
....	....
....	....
....	....
....	....

Next, ask each person to work with another person and each person describes what they see as being creative about the other person.

Finally, ask each person to describe their own personal creative style. This might start with the words given below.

I am creative when I ....

My creativity is at its best when ....

I like to be creative by doing ....

My favourite creative activity is ....

I would like to work on the following attribute ....

People could help me do this by ....

Then ask them to describe themselves using some metaphor that pleases them and that they feel describes their style perfectly. They could also ask their team colleagues to offer a description that they think fits. Have fun doing this.

A Question Of Opposites

One person may be creative because they are impatient, another because they are patient. One because they are bold, another because they are cautious. Whatever our personality or our personal characteristics we can all be creative. It is sometimes just a question of opposites that might open the windows of our creativity.

Much of what has been said in this book is about seeking new and different ways of experiencing the world around us. We can all do it. It helps enormously if we are aware of how we are, or are not creative at the present time.

Conclusion

Whatever your creative style might be, it is yours and yours alone and it is right for you. Finding and developing your creative style can be challenging, exciting and fun. I would encourage you to start now and to continue to seek every possible opportunity to explore and develop your creativity. And be careful when you wake the sleeping giant within you, because there are certain to be plenty of fireworks.

Chapter 16

Business As Unusual

Introduction

One of my great delights in working in organizations is that by using the telescope of creativity, and becoming aware of and focusing on what is happening, however mundane it might seem, perspectives and attitudes shift. It is this aspect of creativity that is 'business as unusual'.

The ability to see things that others cannot see, to have a different way of looking at the ordinary everyday events and things that we all meet all the time, is the underlying key to being creative. When your creativity is switched on all the time the results can be startling.

Fascination With The Ordinary

To see a World in a Grain of Sand,

And a Heaven in a Wild Flower,

Hold Infinity in the palm of your hand,

And Eternity in an hour.

William Blake

Most of what happens in organizations is very ordinary, so much so that it is taken for granted, goes unquestioned and becomes ingrained in what we refer to as the 'culture'. Being creative means being fascinated with the ordinary. When ordinary events and reactions are focused on with the magnifying glass of fascination, they become transformed into exciting and sometimes deeply meaningful events. Here is an example.

Scenario - Tap, tap, tap

I am working with a small, close-knit team, who are discussing the way forward on an important project, when I notice how one of the members is tapping his pencil on his pad. He seems to be listening intently to the person who is speaking. She has finished speaking.

'What is happening for you right now?' I ask the pencil tapper.

'Nothing,' he says.

'I notice you are tapping your pencil on your pad, what's that about?'

'I don't know,' he replies, stopping tapping.

'Do it some more only stronger,' I suggest. As he is doing it I say. 'What are the words that go with it?' At first there are no words then with each tap a word, 'This - is - the - wrong - way - to - go - this - is - the - wrong - way - to - go - this - is - the - wrong - way - to - go ...'

'Which is the right way then?' I ask him interrupting his tapping.

'Well', he says, looking up 'I think ...' and he embarks on a very clear, concise explanation on why the team should do something different. This is something he has not done before, even though he has often tapped his pencil.

After the meeting the team leader asked me how I knew what was going to happen. I told her I didn't know what was going to happen, I was just fascinated with the pencil tapping.

When we ignore the ordinary, we ignore life. We drift along half-asleep until something extra-ordinary wakes us up, and in this process we miss many opportunities to be highly creative.

Exercise 39 - Nothing is ordinary

Ask each member of your team to find something or some event that they consider ordinary and to look at it and explore it in any way that is different than how they normally would. You can use the following as a guide.

If it is an article, bend down and look at it through your legs. What do you see?

....

....

....

....

....

If it is an event, imagine it happened backwards. How does this change things?

....

....

....

....

....

If it is an article, increase its size tenfold. How does this change what you see and experience?

....

....

....

....

....

If it is an event, stop it halfway through and change it in any way you want to. What happens?

....

....

....

....

....

If it is an article, reduce its size tenfold. What do you see now?

....

....

....

....

....

Discovering The Obvious

I have just returned with my dog Jenny from a walk in the woods that surround my home. For the whole of the walk Jenny is darting here and there sniffing and poking with her front paw at the undergrowth. Nothing is obvious to her, everything has to be explored, she never knows what she might turn up.

It has been a beautiful day and the colours of the leaves are wonderful. I stop when I come across some fungus growing on an old tree stump. I am fascinated. I take some photographs and I poke about around the tree stump disturbing some ants that are hurrying along in a military column, each carrying a piece of leaf approximately 10 times its size. For a short time I become lost in this microworld, then Jenny impatient to continue sticks her tongue in my ear.

Have you ever noticed how when someone tells you something is obvious though it doesn't seem to you that it is, but once it has been pointed out to you it becomes obvious?

Have you ever been given directions to find somewhere and you are given some landmark with the fatal words: 'It's obvious you can't miss it.' And what happens? You miss it!

What seems to happen is that the constant babble of thoughts that clutter our minds for most of the time obscure or deaden the information we are receiving from our senses. We are so busy 'thinking' (paying attention to thoughts) that we miss the obvious messages from our senses. Our eyes see the landmark and feed the information to the brain, where it then seems to have to wait for a gap in the babble. By which time we are well past the landmark.

To discover the obvious, we have to pay attention to our senses and listen to what they are telling us. We have to still our frenetic minds and make contact with our environment and other people through our senses. And to make contact with ourselves through our feelings. We have to pay attention and then, and only then, we will discover the obvious.

The Unseen (Because We Don't Look)

I watched the young shop assistant stacking loaves on to the shelf. I waited. She saw me and smiled and carried on stacking the shelf until she had finished. After a few moments she came over to me.

'Can I help you?'

'You could've helped me a few minutes ago. I thought customer service was a priority here,' I said a little impatiently.

'You're right,' she said, 'I'm sorry.'

This is an example of the unseen. The shop assistant saw me, but not my discomfort or my need to be served. She didn't see these other things because she wasn't looking. It was almost as if what she was doing and her focus on that activity was blinding her to my needs.

Have you ever heard the expression: 'That is blindingly obvious.' It is a strange expression, but very perceptive because it is saying that something is so clear that we can't see it. It is as if we are blinded by a veil of thought.

It is not difficult to learn to look and to really take in what we see, not just the physical aspects, but the other aspects of what is happening around us. A heightened level of awareness might be a good way to describe this kind of looking.

The Unheard (Because We Don't Listen)

I was at a meeting about a new series of books I am working on. During the meeting we were discussing the authors' brief that we would be sending to prospective authors for the series. I made what I believed was an important comment.

'I don't like the chapter structure that you have included in the brief. I think it gives authors the wrong impression of what we want.'

The editor replied: 'I don't want to change the brief again. We'll see how we get on with it as it is.'

'I'm sorry,' I said, 'but I think it is important.'

'Well, let me have your ideas in writing after the meeting,' he responded. And we moved on.

I sent my ideas the next day.

Some time later, after receiving several unsatisfactory proposals from authors that had been prepared according to the brief that I didn't like, we had another discussion. The result was that the editor agreed to change the brief in line with my suggestions. And, of course, a lot of time had been wasted.

What happened at the earlier meeting was that for some reason the editor didn't 'hear' what I was saying. His thoughts may have been on something else or perhaps he didn't pay sufficient attention to what I was saying because it didn't fit into the current focus of what he wanted to hear. I call this the 'ear plugs of thought', and it is a very common occurrence in many organizations.

Learning to listen means stilling the constant mind babble and focusing our attention on the person who is speaking, and on what is being said. By focusing on the person first, and seeing them, we are able to hear them clearly. We cannot choose what we hear, unless we use ear plugs, but we can choose what we pay attention to, and listening is all about paying attention.

The Unsaid (Because We Don't Speak)

Perhaps this is one aspect of 'business as unusual' that most frequently generates surprise in people. I think it is because we all choose to censor what we say to such an extent that we often say nothing. Now censoring has its uses, and I am not suggesting that we should never censor. What I am suggesting is that most of us experience moments when we wish 'we had said something'.

One of my favourite interventions with individuals and groups is, 'What really interests me is what you are **not** saying.' Another favourite intervention used by one of my Gestalt trainers is: 'Think out loud.' The aim is to bring the unspoken into the field, because it's only when this happens that we can pay attention to it. If it stays part of your mental babble, it gets lost.

The expression 'tongue-tied' is another of those interesting uses of language. Who ties our tongue so that we cannot speak? It also implies that we know what we want to say, but we can't bring ourselves to say it.

One of the ways that we can realize our unspoken words is to preface what we say with the simple statement, 'What I want you to hear is ...' This simple phrase is like a key to unlock a veritable treasure chest of feelings, ideas, beliefs, emotions, and whatever else you want to set free. The statement is also a powerful way of alerting others to the need I have for them to listen to what I am going to say.

Exercise 40 - The unseen, the unheard, the unsaid

Here is a risky exercise for you to try with your team. Ask your team members including yourself to prepare on their own using the following guide. Then bring them together and discuss the 'hidden obvious'.

What I don't see because I don't look is:

....

....

....

....

What I don't hear because I don't listen is:

....

....

....

....

What I don't say because I stay quiet is:

....

....

....

....

Our Authentic Creative Selves

To be able to operate on the basis of 'business as unusual' means taking risks. All these risks are to do with revealing our truly creative selves to those with whom we come into contact. This is like removing the layers of ourselves from our superficial surface to that deeper, more real level of who we are, like peeling an onion. It is risky because we might get hurt, we might be misunderstood, we might be ridiculed or we might be rejected.

Being creative and authentic means being 'all of me'. This is much more difficult than it sounds and takes a willingness to experiment with removing some of the blocks to our natural process. Leaving my armour, my sword and my shield at home when I venture out into the world. If we do this, it is possible for us to allow ourselves the luxury of being 'fascinated by the ordinary' and the time to 'discover the obvious'.

Conclusion

Being fascinated with the ordinary and discovering the obvious means carrying the telescope of creativity with us wherever we go. This is a magical telescope that can increase or reduce the size of things, it can help us to see things that other people don't see. The key to using the telescope of creativity is to open our eyes, our ears, our mouths and our hearts and to let the fascinating world in.

Chapter 17

Creativity Notebook

Introduction

This notebook is provided for you and your team to monitor and learn about your own individual creativity. My suggestion is that each person creates their own personal 'creativity notebook' in the form of the one provided in this chapter.

Using Your Creative Notebook

There are five sections in the notebook:

- Creative thoughts and ideas
- How my creativity is blocked
- Experimenting with being creative
- Risks I am taking and want to take
- Defining and understanding my own creativity

In each of these sections your 'creativity notebook' offers ideas and suggestions for how you can keep a record of and work consciously at being creative. After all, no matter how hard I try to convince you of the importance of being creative, it is entirely up to you how and when you tap your own creativity.

I hope your 'creativity notebook' helps.

Creative thoughts and ideas

Give your thoughts and ideas a name and draw a picture or create a collage from cut-outs from magazines that will give you a colourful visualization of your idea.

IDEA Name ....

Description

....

....

....

....

....

How I can make this happen is by

....

....

....

....

....

IDEA Name ....

Description

....

....

....

....

....

....

How I can make this happen is by

....

....

....

....

....

....

(Photocopy this page to record as many more ideas as you may have whenever they may occur to you.)

Now list your creative thoughts and ideas and incubate where you are up to with them by putting a tick in the appropriate column.

Ideas name	Record data	Incubate	Recognize spark	Refine	Take action
1					
2					
3					
4					
5					
6					
7					
8					

How my creativity is blocked

In Chapter 9 we looked at the nine uncreative boxes that are ways in which we block our creativity. There was also an exercise about owning your particular uncreative box.

This section of your 'creativity notebook' is for you to record instances when you have blocked your creativity under the headings of the nine creative boxes plus an extra box for your very own creative invention of how you stop your creativity. Make a note of what happened on each occasion you blocked your creativity and what you did about it.

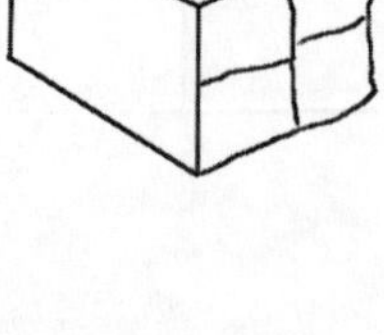

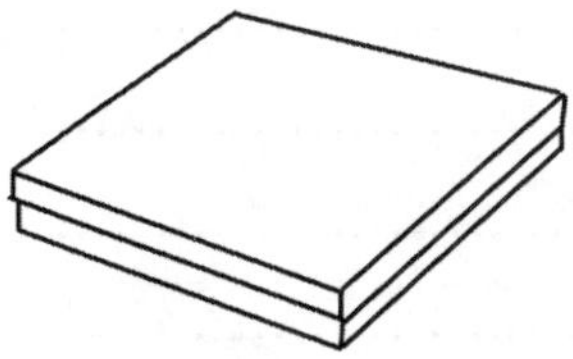

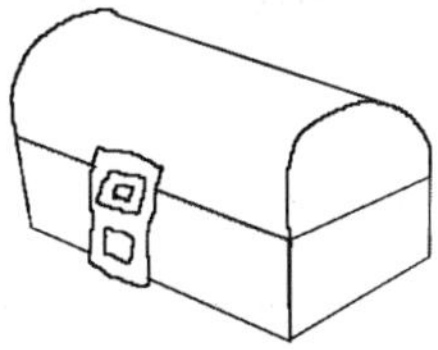

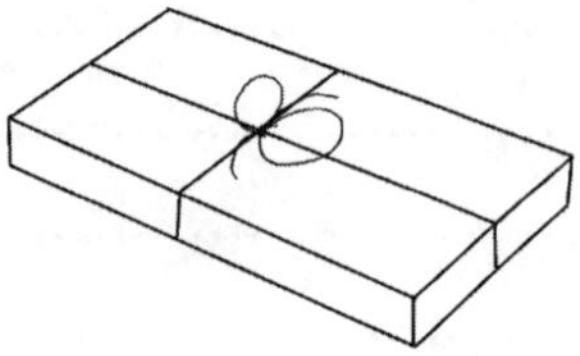

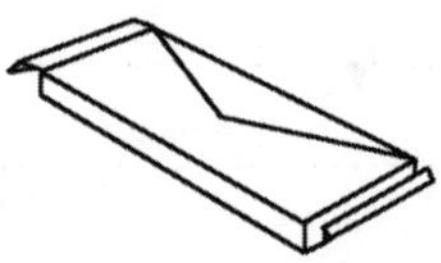

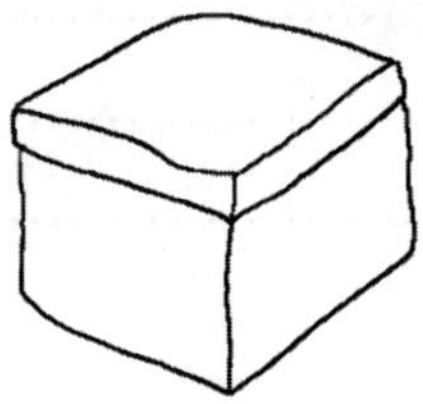

The last uncreative box is your very own which you have invented and which you can now name and describe.

Experimenting with being creative

Record your creative experiments below.

Experiment 1

Description

....

....

....

What happened?

....

....

....

....

What did you do?

....

....

....

Experiment 2

Description

....

....

....

What happened?

....

....

....

....

What did you do?

....

....

....

(Photocopy this page to record more experiments.)

Risks I am taking and want to take

In Chapter 3 we looked at the idea of balancing risks and creating your own 'risk continuum' from low risk to high risk. This is a chance to record the risks you are taking and the risks you want to take.

Risks I am taking

Risk 1 Description

....

....

....

What's the pay off?

....

....

....

What's the worst that could happen?

....

....

....

Risk 2 Description

....

....

....

What's the pay off?

....

....

....

What's the worst that could happen?

....

....

....

(Photocopy this page to record more risks that you are taking.)

Risks I want to take

Risk W1 Description

....

....

....

What would the pay off be?

....

....

....

What's the worst that could happen?

....

....

What is stopping me?

....

....

Risk W2 Description

....

....

....

What would the pay off be?

....

....

....

What's the worst that could happen?

....

....

What is stopping me?

....

....

(Photocopy this page to record more risks that you want to take.)

Defining and understanding your own creativity

Attach a current photograph of yourself in the space below.

I am a creative person because I

....

....

....

....

....

....

....

....

....

I have a preference for left-brain/right-brain activities (underline the one that applies mostly to you, or both if you feel you fully integrate your left and right brain).

Record in the boxes below the activities that you enjoy that

fit into each category.

Left Brain	Right Brain

Remember these divisions are only a guide to help you understand more about your own creativity.

Most people have certain aspects of being creative that they really enjoy and look forward to, what are yours?

What I enjoy about being creative is:

Give some examples of how you do this:

Many people actively dislike certain aspects of being creative, what are the aspects you dislike?

What I dislike and avoid about being creative is:

Give some examples of when you have avoided being creative:

You can add to both these sections as you discover more about your creativity.

Where would you put yourself on the creativity continuum?

Highly imaginative and creative most of the time ....

....

....

....

....

Quite often creative ....

....

....

....

....

Sometimes creative ....

....

....

....

....

Rarely creative ....

....

....

....

....

Never creative ....

....

....

....

....

Write down some way that you could move up the continuum, if indeed you want to. If you are already at the 'highly imaginative' end, write below how you could encourage and support others to be more creative.

....

....

....

....

....

....

....

List below 10 things you could do in the next few weeks to be more creative.

1. ....
2. ....
3. ....
4. ....
5. ....
6. ....
7. ....
8. ....
9. ....
10. ....

Conclusion

I hope that you have found this book both an enjoyable and a creative experience and that you feel encouraged to be creative. Enjoy your future creativity

SUGGESTED READING

Adams, James L. (I 986) *The Care and Feeding of Ideas: A Guide to Encouraging Creativity*, Addison-Wesley, Reading, MA.

Barker, Joel (1992) *Future Edge*, William Morrow, New York.

de Bono, Edward (1992) *Six Thinking Hats*, Little, Brown & Company, New York.

Drucker, Peter F. (1985) *Innovation and Entrepreneurship*, Harper & Row, New York.

Gross, T. Scott (1991) *Positively Outrageous Service*, Master-media, New York.

Handy, Charles (1990) *The Age of Unreason*, Harvard Business School Press, Boston, MA.

Hanks, Kurt and Ja A. Parry (1994) *Wake Up Your Creative Genius*, William Kaufmann, CA.

Higgins, James M. (I994) *101 Creative Problem Solving Techniques*, New Management Publishing, Flo.

Mattimore, Bryan W. (1993) *99% Inspiration*, AMACOM, New York.

Michalko, Michael (1991) *Thinkertoys*, Ten Speed Press, CA.

Noble, Sara (ed.) (I991) *Great Management Ideas from America's Most Innovative Small Companies*, Inc. Publishing, MA.

Ray, Michael and Rochelle Myers (1986) *Creativity in Business*, Doubleday, New York.

von Oech, Roger (1983) *A Whack in the Side of the Head*, Harper & Row, New York.

von Oech, Roger (1986) *A Kick in the Seat of the Pants*, Harper & Row, New York.